To the Monsters

You are a wound, not a healing wound, not a wound surgically placed for future use or repair. You are a horrible accident that rips open the flesh of the innocent. You are inflamed, infected, oozing, and disgusting. Your stink is that of stagnant, dark, swarmed, shallow water. You hurt, you damage, you cause fear and anxiety. You are never treated, so you never go away. You are ever present, a reminder—a reminder of the past, of evil, of complete and utter indecency.

There is no cure; you're a wound that is only treated with jabs of sharp instruments and salt. You last a lifetime; you cause embarrassment and anger. You paralyzed me, you handicapped me, you caused a disability for which there was no rehabilitation. No medication, no stiches, no gauze could ever close up and heal the deep lacerations I bear.

I am not your only victim. I am just one of many—one of the many small children in which you sank your claws, let your evil escape through, one of many who will never forget you. You are a predator, a depiction of the lack of humanity, the result of a godless soul. You weep with selfishness and smell of regret, sadness, hopelessness.

My power comes in revelation. You will be revealed. We see you; we sense the darkness within. You are well rehearsed; you know the language, the charisma, and the charm in order to make your way in. But the mark is there. The scars run deep, and we recognize the evil.

We will not stay your prey. We will not let the damage you initiated continue to our deaths. We will not let you consume both our bodies and our souls. We will forgive not for your sake but for ours. We will never forget, but that memory will be used as a warning and not a crutch. We will take back our power and finally heal.

To My Mother

For decades, you were to blame. You did not know how to be a mother. You birthed babies but did not nurture them. You did not protect them; you set them free too early. You lacked the affection, that motherly instinct that you read about in books when the mama bear defends her cubs. We were defenseless for the longest time. I often wondered why you kept us, why you did not just kill in utero, because what was the point of birthing unloved, unwanted children? The result filled me with insecurities and extreme fear. I did not have you to count on or confide in. I spent so much time filled with bitterness and hatred for you. You sacrificed our relationship, and for that, I was incredibly hurt.

I had seen too much, been through too much, and been damaged to the core. I needed you to be there for me, to speak up, and to stop the monsters who tried to destroy me. Instead, you ignored me, neglected me, and left me to wolves. I had every right to feel disowned, dishonored, and disregarded. You ignored my needs and looked at me as an inconvenience. You were purposely blind to the pain I suffered. You were caught up in your own selfishness and your own salvation that anything that happened around you did not even matter in your sight. You were to blame. You were to blame for the beatings, for the rapes, for the unwanted touches, and for the love I never received. You did not show me how to be a respectable, confident, strong woman. Instead, you showed me everything that I did not want to be.

You were a product of the past. A curse that lay within your mom was passed to you and shown in me. How could you love a daughter when you were a daughter unloved? You didn't know how to break those chains or reverse that curse. You instead prayed for your saving and didn't feel you could reach for me at the same time. You were one-minded, caught, and tangled; your lack of multitasking showed.

For the same reasons I hated you, I also related to you. Once I found out that you came from the same pain I did, that you knew nothing good as a child, it eventually gave me a different perspective. It took a lot of time, an incredible amount of damage and tears, but I have come to forgive your mistakes and appreciate that we started over. Through the lack of mothering, you were able to become my friend and a sister through Christ. I accept you for who you are and forgive what you have done.

To My Children

I pray with all my heart that you have learned to forgive me. As you have grown, you have come to know more about me than I have known myself. I am deeply saddened by the pain and trauma that my past has caused you. I hope that through the horror, you are able to see the unconditional love I have for you. The only reason I have fought to survive is because of you.

I honestly tried my best to be a good mom; this is why you saw me rise and fall so many times. I know I lacked the skills to be an outgoing, positive, and loving mother. I let the demons defeat me in so many circumstances that it made me feel that I wasn't worthy of your love or the opportunity of this world. My heart aches that I was not there for you all the way I intended to be. I cannot stand the fact that I let abuse, men, and drugs get in the way of a relationship that you needed. I genuinely did everything in my power at that time to make things work. It kills me that so much of my joy and competence were stolen from me and that you paid the price. I cannot say sorry enough, and I cannot erase the past no matter how much I wish I could. All I can do is hope and pray that you find peace within yourself and toward me for my mistakes. Please don't hold that hate, please do not hold those burdens because they are heavy and they dig a hole deep inside you that will tarnish anything good in your life.

My hope for you is that you learn through my mistakes and that you profit from my misfortune. I know that the pain that I have experienced did not go in vain as long as it prevents you from feeling the same type of pain. I hope that you have learned that you can survive and that with the love of God, anything and everything is possible. Through my weaknesses, I hope you have grown strong.

I am sure that by now you are aware that no one is perfect, but the good intentions are there. Know that through every battle, God is with you and you cannot give up. We are all stubborn, but we are fighters. We make mistakes, but we can recognize them, ask for forgiveness, and refuse to let them dictate our future. As God forgives our transgressions, we must forgive one another.

What Are Your Earliest Memories?

That is usually the question by many psychologists and therapists when trying to get to the root of trauma. My first memory is that of the pain of winter. I hated the biting feeling of Wisconsin winter winds against my unprotected skin, the aching that hit your fingers first and made its way to the rest of your body. My brothers and I were always the ones feeling the pain; our tears and whining went unnoticed by our mother's ears. I remember wondering why other mommies took the time to put their babies in hats, gloves, scarves when my mommy didn't.

I remember noticing that other little girls and boys had a daddy at home. We didn't have a daddy; all we had was Mommy, and she was never around. I wondered why we didn't have a daddy and how we could get one. What made us so bad that a daddy didn't want to be around? What was so awful that Mommy was never home? Mommy didn't say "I love you" like other mommies. There were no questions, no hugs, no kisses, and no words of encouragement. I asked why a lot: Why don't we have a real mommy or daddy? Why did my grandma hate my mommy like Mommy hates us? My baby brother, Redd; my younger brother, Sam; and I had to look out for one another. We had to comfort one another when one was hurt or scared. We had to forget about our pain and sadness fast; there was no time to feel.

A life of filth—my mommy had a collection, a collection of stuff, piles of clothing, maybe clean, mostly dirty, piled basically ceiling high in the corners of the house we were in. We made a game of jumping on the mountains and crawling through the paths of forgotten socks, books, dishes, and rotting food. Strangers were dropping off more garbage, and my mommy was bringing home more boxes of forgotten, unwanted stuff to her forgotten, unwanted children. My room was the cleanest; I had to make it that way. The piles of stuff, the mice, and the bugs made me feel crazy. When we took in a pregnant cat and she had her kittens, I made sure she had them in my room, as far away from the filth as I could get them. We were part of the garbage, left to fend for ourselves, left to rot. I would fight—fight in school constantly. Other kids were mean to my brothers and me. They would make fun of our dirty hair, our smell, and the holes in our used clothing. Anger was fed at school. There was no learning, there was no relaxing, there were no friends or fun. Everywhere I went was a battle. I was constantly defending the horrible names and insults cast upon me and my family. Embarrassed to raise my hand, I would cringe at the thought of eyes staring at me or whispers in the room.

Embarrassment—at that time, I didn't know that this was the feeling I would get when Mommy would force us to go to church every Sunday filthy. She never cleaned anything, including her children. I would see all the other people at church clean, smelling good, in hats, dresses, shiny shoes, and pressed suits. My brothers and I dug up what we could out of the mixed piles of clothing to make sure we were dressed on time to leave. I once heard about how Jesus loves children. Love? Could I possibly find love in this place? Love that I never knew even existed? This made me excited to go, but embarrassment eventually would curse that excitement.

I was told that Jesus loved us. My mother did not. Mommy went to church all the time, mostly without us. She would scream at us when we were bad or made mistakes about how we were going to burn in hell. I heard other people make fun of her. She was the "holy roller" or "Jesus freak." People of the church consumed her mind and time. She made me cringe with embarrassment when she would condemn people that she just met. The only moments she took the time to talk to us, it was about the Rapture. It was stories of fear, doom, and apocalypse. The fear of Jesus returning to earth and only taking those who were good in his eyes and leaving everyone else behind to kill, rape, and abuse one another was the story that began to rattle my young conscience. We lived in an environment of constant terror and tremulous relationships. There were many nights when Mommy was at church or Bible study and was hours late. I would hold my brothers tight in anticipation that Jesus took my mommy and left us garbage kids behind. We screamed and cried in one another's arms many times. In our fear, I became the leader. Even though Redd was older than me, I nurtured and tried my best to protect both of my brothers.

Redd was different. He was strong yet very vulnerable. I had a strong sense of protection over him. He didn't have a lot of other people for friends, and he hung out with girls instead of other little boys. He didn't play sports or wrestle like the other boys. He was made fun of unbearably, taunted and tormented at school, being called a girl and faggot. It infuriated me. It lit a fire in me that blazed so strong that my small body couldn't contain it and I had to let it escape through my fists. These outbursts of pain happened multiple times, sometimes on my own behalf, but mostly for my brothers. Over time, we knew that we only had one another. We only had one another to count on, to protect us. No one understood us, everyone ignored our pain; only we knew what dreadful things we had waiting for us.

Pain

Pain is a very familiar emotion. It's the only feeling I recognized for a long time. I knew pain before other feelings in my life. It was not always physical, but I felt it. Pain and I were best friends for a long time. I knew it when I heard it. And I heard it the worst from Redd. I woke up, and he was screaming in pain. I heard the lashing, thrashing, whips of a belt, and yes, Redd was screaming. It was Mommy. Mommy was beating Redd. Why? Why did Redd make Mommy think of hate? When Redd jumped rope, played games, wore girls' clothes, or said things that girls would say, Mommy despised him. As we were growing up, it didn't take long to know that Redd was gay. It didn't take long to find out that Redd had a different daddy from the rest of us. It didn't take long to know that whoever Redd's daddy was, it made Mommy enraged, and Redd took the result. Mommy would scream at Redd, scream and yell about living in sin and him being an atrocity to God's eyes. Everything Redd did, Mommy loathed over and chastised him for it. Redd acted out more and more; he didn't care if he got beaten. He would skip church and school, left the house whenever he wanted. He no longer feared punishment. Sam and I followed. School and church became a place of disgrace, and making those places a priority was the furthest thing from our minds.

We became street children, running around all day only to return at night to sleep. We were forgotten; it didn't matter. We found other kids in the same situations as us; we indulged. We began to experiment with alcohol and the occasional joint. I had a taste of numbness, of delirium and began a love affair with it. The substances and I would flirt; it pampered me, wrapped me in a warm, comfortable blanket, and helped me forget the worries of my world. As time would go on, this flirtatious affair would become a relationship that I should have never entertained, a marriage that I should have annulled, an obsession that would take a miracle to conquer.

Monsters

As a child, when you have a nightmare, you are engulfed. You are transcended into a horror movie in which you are the only victim. You are at the mercy of the monster. The plot is already written, but you never read the script. Everything is an unexpected, bewildering event. At least in a nightmare, it ends. Usually, a mommy comes in your room and comforts you. She is supposed to hug you, kiss you, and tell you everything is okay. She is supposed to rescue you from the torment you were going through and take you away from the monster who haunted you. Throughout life, those nightmares were real. Those monsters existed, and Mommy wasn't there to rescue me.

Monsters are not human. They may look like people. They walk, talk, and dress like everyone else, but this is the exterior that they take on in order to blend in. They have to blend in. If someone saw a monster coming, they would surely hide. I would have hidden. I would not speak to them; I would see them for what they were and escape from their presence immediately. That is their trick; they blend, and they blend well. They study others and mimic their mannerisms. They act like good daddies and mommies. They go to church, they pray with the other people, they dance and sing like everyone else. They open their Bibles, pretending to learn, acting like studying. It's not long before you realize that God could not exist there. Their insides are too dark and thick that no Holy Spirit could ever penetrate those souls. Kids are always comforted that monsters don't exist, but they do. They are not hiding under your bed. They are living next door or sitting in the next church pew.

Mommy knew a lot of monsters. Most of these people went to church. These people are supposed to be good people. People who go to church every Sunday, attend events, and hold Bible studies are supposed to be loving and compassionate. These are the people you go to for help or prayer. These are the people that God is supposed to use to show His forgiveness, for His love and for His affection. These people are the people that Mommy thought she was leaving me with. Some of these people were liars. Some of these people used God's love as a cover. These certain people didn't attend church to grow closer to God; they attended church to atone for the ugliest that was inside of them. These certain people had smiles on their faces but evil in their eyes. They spoke deceit and manipulation. They went through the motions, spoke the words they were supposed to say, and went to the venues where they can show face and maintain a reputation. These people were hypocrites. These people had such a darkness in them that it had to escape through innocent victims. These people were the people Mommy would leave us with, and the victims were her own children.

One of the "friends" Mommy had was Sue. Sue was funny looking to me. She was a really large woman. She was the biggest woman I had ever seen, so when I saw her at church, other kids and I would point, giggle, and tell jokes about her. I first saw her at the local community center where Mommy would take us for free food and games. We would be playing in the activity room and playing with Sue's kids.

Sue suggested we come to her house and play sometime. My mommy was too enthusiastic to oblige. Sue stayed in the blue room. It was like no other room I had ever seen. The walls were painted with a baby blue, there was blue carpeting, and all the furniture in the room varied in different shades of blue. Sue lay stationary on the blue sofa, rarely ever moving, as we kids would play. We weren't allowed to bother her too much or enter the blue room. This is where I met Butch. Butch lived with Sue. He was a scary-looking huge man. He was incredibly intimidating. His menacing eyes would meet mine, and I would immediately be forced to look away and try my hardest to pretend he wasn't there. Butch didn't say too much in the beginning. In the beginning, he catered to Sue's needs, fetching the food, phone, or whatever other necessity she needed. After a few visits, Butch showed more interest in our activities, more specifically mine.

During these visits, Sue paid less attention to us and Butch paid more; other kids from the neighborhood would come over and hang out. His house became another party house where other kids who had mommies like mine could escape. Butch began to give us malt liquor and would force us to drink it as fast as we could. I felt sick, dizzy, heavy, and out of control. Butch set up fights. He became my trainer. He would make me fight the other kids and force me to beat them as hard as I could.

In training, I had to be strong. I had to drink that alcohol as fast as I could and as much as I could and let the aching that was inside of me come out in rage. Butch punched me in my stomach and hit me over and over in order to toughen me up. I cried the first few times, but it was not long before he taught me how to shove that pain and embarrassment away. It was not long before his beatings did not hurt as bad as they did in the beginning. It was not long before I became a violent, out-of-control child who bottled up all the aggression just to take it out on the faces of other kids. He promised that if I did not perform the way he wanted me to, he would punish me worse. He found it entertaining, whooping and hollering as drunken young kids had a fistfight in front of him. He would sometimes bring his friends over, and they would drink alcohol and root for us to punch harder, to stop crying and get up. Over time, gradually, my brothers didn't go over to Sue and Butch's house as often. It didn't take long before they refused to visit.

The fighting hurt physically, but it made me feel special. Someone took the time to talk to me, to spend time with me, to show me attention. I did what I could to please Butch. On one hand, I wanted to make me proud, but more importantly, I was afraid of him. One time, when I was about to go home, Butch told me that the next time I came over, I should wear a dress. He wanted us to look nice so we could take pictures. He wanted a picture of me. This was new attention that I was deprived of for so long; therefore, I was excited. I wanted to look nice; I wanted my picture taken. The next visit, I followed the directions given and wore a dress. Butch was extra attentive to me. He commented about how nice I looked and that I should wear dresses more often. The entire time was spent sitting on his lap as he demanded. I sat wondering why the middle of his lap was swollen and pressing on me. He continued by rubbing my legs with his rough hands. I felt awkward and strange, at the same time trying to act normal so that he didn't think anything was wrong. As he put his hands on my thighs and me on his lap, he made me pose for the pictures he took. He would tell me I was pretty more often and continued to train me for fighting. He was able to tap into a whole other fury in me when he would pretend that my opponent for the moment just killed my mommy. Although my mommy was not a good person to me, Butch was able to use the protector in me to induce physical agony on others.

Butch's touching became more forceful. Once he started putting fingers inside of me, the threats became real. He countlessly warned me not to tell anyone, and if I made noise or tried to scream or cry, I'd bother Sue, and she would be mad at me. Mommy was always mad at me, and I didn't want to make anyone else mad. I would consume the liquor he provided and pass out only to waken in a daze in the blue room and bottomless. Sue had had surgery to lose weight, which caused her to not be around as much. Complications from the surgery eventually killed her. I recall going to her funeral and seeing the giant-sized casket with her massive, lifeless body in it. I went up to the casket with the other visitors and could have sworn that I saw her eyelids twitch. I stood there in anticipation, waiting for her eyes to flash open, but they never did. Sue was officially gone, and Butch no longer had her to linger around the house and inconvenience his plans.

Bob was an old war veteran who lived down the street. He had a small dog and lived above a Laundromat. He was always seen outside with his dog and talking to the kids of the neighborhood. My brothers and I would join other kids we knew to go to his house and get beer, cigarettes, and weed. He would host a multitude of parties at his house. He would get us all to indulge as much as we needed to in getting high and drunk. Once we were inebriated enough, he would force some of us to take a bath. During these baths, he would touch us, paying special attention to our privates. Bob was usually not very violent. He would give us anything he could in order to be able to perform sexual acts on us. He too took pictures of the things we did and what we did with one another. I found a shoebox under his sink filled with photos of kids naked and having sex, including myself. My mind was already damaged from Butch taking advantage of me that Bob's advances were something I felt I could tolerate. He performed oral sex on both the little boys and girls who ended up at his house. In exchange, we got all the weed, cigarettes, and booze that we wanted to fill the void that outside monsters were hollowing out. He forced a few of us to pose in sexual acts on each other while he took pictures. I thought this was the role that every little girl has with men. I felt ugly on the inside, but I knew no other relationship with men. I did not have a daddy to tell me how to act like a young lady; my mommy never acknowledged that I was alive, let alone add any value to my self-worth. Bob showed affection under the disgusting things he did, and that was what I looked for. I wanted to be doted over and shown attention, so I got it however I could get it. Everyone at Bob's parties knew the party was over when Bob had a lot to drink and began telling, reminiscing about war. His entire face would change; his demeanor became violent. He was incredibly scary when he started to speak about various stories. I knew that was my cue to pack it up and escape. He would die soon after, and all I could think about, all I still think about is, What happened to the pictures—the pictures of lost souls, the collection he kept? Who saw them? Did anyone recognize me? Who has their hands on evidence of my horror? It haunts me still.

I knew that what these old adult men were doing to me was wrong. Every touch, every look and act haunted me. It began a slow rot to my soul. I would cringe when it was happening, but it was not long before it didn't feel like it was happening to me. Most of the time, I was filled with alcohol and drugs to help numb my body and silence my mind. I stepped away from that little girl's body; I blacked out the ugly and tried everything I could to bury it away. The numbness seeped its way into my entire life. As much as I did it to not feel pain, I also could not feel love. I did not know what it felt like to receive true, unconditional love. I did not know what it felt like to be cared about and protected. Mommy was never around for the pain, and she never was around to give the love. This made it difficult to show love to others. I built an impenetrable wall around my emotions, around my heart and soul. I began to become hard stone because I knew that people were bad and it was only a matter of time before they did what they wanted to me and took from me whatever they desired.

The things these people did to me made me question God even more. Even from this young age, I talked to God, begged God. I begged for His love and forgiveness. These things were obviously happening because I was bad. I obsessed whether or not I was worthy of God's love. My own mommy didn't love me, so how could He? If He knew my every move, if He knew what I had done with these men, If He knew about the drugs I was doing and the alcohol I was consuming, how could He possibly still love me? I fell under this spell, the spell of worthlessness. I had no value; I was used up and emptied out. I tried to be someone I was not. I tried to be good, smart; I tried to go to school like the normal boys and girls. I felt anything but normal. I was outlasted and thrown away. I was at the will of savages, the prey of wolves. An innocent little girl was thrown to grown men to do with what they pleased. I screamed and begged God for a way out. I pleaded for a savior to come in, hold me in their arms, and carry me away from the hell I was engulfed in. I lost my way; I lost my will. I gave up my personality, my strength. It took all of me just to survive. It took all of me to find somewhere in my mind to go and shut the door while horrible acts were done to me. I had to check out. The things I did and the things that were done to me soon didn't seem like they twirled in the same mind or body. Patches of memory soon disappeared. If I denied it, ignored it, never acknowledging it, did it really happen?

Once Sue was gone for sure, Butch had nothing to stop him from having me all to himself. He forced me to put my mouth on him, and he put his mouth on me. He played the same songs over and over while making me dance naked. I, to this day, cannot stand to hear those songs. Those songs bring back those memories, those feelings, and I can feel the anger and fear swirl uncontrollably inside of me. The first time he entered me felt like a scorching sword searing my insides and ripping me apart. I dared not to scream. Silent tears stained my flushed cheeks as I prayed for him to just finish. That would be a constant prayer for me. I just wanted it to be finished. My coping mechanism was drinking and drugs; they helped me escape. I was able to escape Butch, that blue room, Bob, and Mommy all by ingesting whatever substances were available. It was the only thing I could do to try to survive. Being naked around Butch or Butch being naked around me no longer became an awkward situation. Sadly, it became normal. He kept me in his bed as he slept after he used me up. When someone knocked on the door, I would wake him up and throw his clothes at him in order to answer. I was captive in his sick sexual prison. I was scared for my life and for the lives of my mommy and brothers if I did not comply. If he could do this to me without batting an eye, then I knew he wouldn't hesitate to hurt my family. I would tremble at his threats and vomit regret after his assaults on me. Among the threats on my family, Butch also threatened me with death. At that time, I did not completely understand death. The vision of Sue's dead body stained my memory for life, and Butch threatened that Sue would come back for me and take me if I did not do what he wanted. I did not understand that dead people could not come back, so the vision of this undead person stalking me scared me to my core.

I wanted someone to notice, anyone. I would leave my bloody underwear in the bathroom for Mommy to find, and when she did, she asked what was going on. When I was too scared to actually tell her, she didn't ask again. I had multiple temper tantrums; I had an internal fire that was searing me so bad I had to let it out. I stopped traffic while crossing the street with Mommy, lay in the middle of the street, and screamed and cried. I screamed at the top of my lungs and scratched my face in frustration. Why didn't she care? She knew something awful was happening to her daughter, but she was unwilling to do anything. She was so preoccupied being "saved" and fellowshipping with her church friends that she didn't have the concern for anything that was an inconvenience. I had violent outbursts at home toward my mommy and my brothers. I would run into Mommy's room in the middle of the night, ball up my fists, and hit her just like Butch showed me to. I hated her; I despised her. I picked up knives and tried to cut them. I screamed, cried, and begged for Mommy not to leave us all the time. I hated when she took us by the homes of strangers because we would fall asleep after her long visits only to find out she had left us there. I was rescued, but not for a long time, and I was rescued from Butch by a stranger. It was my mother who finally came to the house and demanded me home, but it was a stranger who called her and told her that if she wanted to see me alive, she'd better come get me. She snatched me out of his grip, and I never saw him again. I wondered who took my place after I left. How many other kids remember how his voice sounded when he cursed or how his heavy body felt on top of them? How many kids were beaten? How many other innocent souls were desecrated and tossed to this wolf?

The pain of embarrassment and yearning for love made itself clear when I met one of Mommy's friends from church, Kay. Kay was a nice lady. Her house was clean, neat, and fresh smelling. She had four boys and no daughters, so she made me feel so special when I visited. She took us horseback riding. I fell in love with the freedom and weightless feeling of swimming in her pool. I didn't have to worry about my belly aching for a meal; she fed me plenty. I didn't have to worry about the filth stuck to my clothing or the aroma coming from them because Kay made sure I had clean clothes to wear. Kay had a family; she had a husband, so her boys had a daddy. I got a glimpse of what Mommy should do and fell in love. I craved for someone like that in my life. I felt the pain of envy for the first time. I wanted everything Kay was willing to offer. Mommy never did any of these things for me, and it made me despise her, it made me hate her, and it made me loathe going home with her. Kay inspired me. She decorated her home so beautifully. She had hobbies. She decorated shadow boxes. All her decor was dusted, clean, and shiny. I wanted so desperately to stay in that environment.

This all ended on account of my own doing. The time I was swimming and went to get dressed changed my path. I was in the bathroom midchange and naked. Suddenly, Kay's sons came barging into the bathroom. Two of the boys grabbed my arms, with the other spreading my legs open. I knew another attack was about to happen. I started to escape my body to prepare when Kay heard something going on and came running in the bathroom. She immediately screamed at her sons and grabbed a belt. She beat them relentlessly for what they were intending to do to me. I relished in their punishment. This was the first time someone saved me, stuck up for me. The boys got what they deserved. If only others could have gotten theirs. It didn't take long after this incident for Kay to reconsider my long summers and weekends by her house. She explained to me how growing boys' bodies change and that she didn't feel I was safe at her house. I was no longer allowed by her house. This devastated me. What did I do wrong? I should have been quiet. I should have not made it a big deal. The other men touched me, so what did it matter if these boys did? Kay's house was the only environment that I felt safe and comfortable in; it was my haven. I was being an inconvenience again. I had to be discarded again.

Spending time at Kay's house made me realize just how poor I was and just how dirty Mommy's house was. It made me hate Mommy even more. I didn't understand why Kay was able to be more organized, her kids had chores and rules when Mommy didn't even care whether we were in school or not. Kay gave me a glimpse of what could have been. I could have lived in a glorious, clean environment. I could have gone to school without anxiety or fear of being embarrassed. I could have gone about day after day not feeling the need to cause harm in order to escape my anger. I could have gone to bed every night in my own bed, warm, comfortable, and with my belly full. I could have avoided the pain to come. The introduction to monster after monster would have never occurred. I could have developed into a woman who was a better mommy, wife, and woman. I could have been happier. I felt that I took that opportunity away from myself and that the other people Mommy knew took so much more. I later learned that Kay tried to take me away from Mommy and adopt me on three separate occasions before the incident with her kids. It broke my heart that she wanted me when I was younger, but the older I got and the more broken I became, the burden of raising me made her change her mind. I required a lot of work to fix, and no one was up for that job.

Hypocrites

My life is riddled with people who were bad actors, people who played a role in front of Mommy and others; but deep down, way below the surface, they were filled with darkness. These people are dolls covered in deceit and lies. They are shiny plastic that makes the public admire them and look up to them. Their painted, bright smiles and adoring big eyes are only a cover to investigate their next unsuspecting victim. If you were to break these dolls to see what the inside was made of, they would exude deception and immorality. They work so hard to have these separate lives I often wonder how exhausting it must be.

It has to be so tiring to act for most of the time and completely let the insanity out for a short time. There has to be a storm, a hurricane just waiting to flood the inside of them. It did not take me long to think that this storm was within everyone. No one was genuine; no one was being real. They would just trade in their worn, torn plastic for a new one. What are they really made of? Everything on the outside was false but portrayed nicely. I could not believe anyone, not even Mommy. They were all liars.

Barbara was one of the nicest ladies at church. She was always greeting people, saying hello to the kids. She was helpful, always going to the events and cleaning. Mommy and she had long conversations about Jesus. They went to Bible studies together, went to church together. It didn't take long before Mommy left us with her alone. As Mommy would leave out the door, Barbara's plastic, painted-on smile began to smear into a jagged snarl. Her entire demeanor changed. The love she showed to Mommy and the people at church transformed into hate toward the poor, dirty children that were left in her home. She spewed curses and insults about our clothes, the way we looked, our lack of money. She grabbed me and my brothers, picked us up, and tossed us in an emptied room. We landed on the mattress that was on the floor and watched in terror as she slammed the door and locked it. We would eventually fall asleep after the screaming and crying exhausted us. My brothers and I were petrified to go to Barbara's house. We pleaded with Mommy every time to not go there. She never questioned why we were so upset—anything to rid her of our presence. Barbara had a piano in her home that one of her sons played on. I wanted to play too. I tiptoed up to the piano, and as soon as I placed my tiny fingers on the key, Barbara's shadow covered me. She pulled out the fallboard and slammed it on my hands. I yelped at the throbbing that took over my hands. She grabbed me and shoved me into the worst place, the dark place, her attic. The attic was stifling in the summer and freezing in the winter, complete darkness. It was hell on earth. Once she made the attic a common place for my brothers and me, we began to escape. Once Redd figured out we could get out through a window, we had our escape. We escaped Barbara but only ran into the presence of other predators.

Mommy taking us to visit her friends and leaving us became more and more frequent. We went to the house of Joan, a friend of Mommy's. After horns of conversation, we fell asleep. I was awakened by the familiar, unwanted touches of a sick grown man. I stayed still, fully awake, and once he walked away, I cracked my eyes open. He stood by a window and began to pray out loud. He was asking Jesus for forgiveness. He prayed about demons and fighting an urge. When he would approach me again, I pretended to sleep, and he rubbed my legs, making his way up. Then he would run away again to the window and repeat the same prayers. I was terrified. What else did he plan to do that he needed to talk to God about? After a few times of going back and forth, he began to get more and more aggressive with his touches. The ugly things he was doing did not match the begging that came out of his mouth. How could he keep touching a little girl's privates and immediately be forgiven? Does God work like this? It seemed incredibly evil. Once I felt like jumping out of my skin, I finally popped my eyes open and screamed as loud as I could to wake my brothers up. This startled him. He tried to comfort me. He got my brothers and me together and left me alone until Mommy came back to get us.

Mommy was not so different from Barbara. Mommy never locked us in a room, but she too was plastic. She constantly opened her mouth and said "Jesus," but wasn't Jesus loving? It perplexed me how she knew so much about God but did not know how to show God's love. The preacher would scream about forgiveness. If we just asked for forgiveness, God would forgive, and we would go to heaven. If it's this simple, do the monsters get to go to heaven if they just say sorry? I didn't want to see Bob or Butch in heaven. Everything in church became a question to me. I no longer saw the point in going. Almost everyone there was not who they portrayed to be. The good experiences I did have, I ruined by my own actions. I no longer felt I deserved anything good, I no longer felt I deserved forgiveness, I no longer felt I deserved God's love. Why would God love me? I am tarnished, used up, and repeatedly thrown out. The choir would sing about how Jesus is our father and He loves us like a father. I never had a father. What did that love feel like? Church was confusing. I had so many unanswered questions. They would say one thing, but everything I experienced in life was the total opposite. I drowned the confusion out. Wondering how this all worked just made me ashamed of what I had done. I had fallen into a deep, dark hole, and I didn't have the tools to get myself out. The only escape was drugs and alcohol. I would fill myself up so that when things were done to me, so when I woke up with my pants off, I did not remember why or what happened. I didn't care; I became stone.

Missing Family

My heart ached for a family. I saw other families, and it filled me with jealousy. I wanted a mommy who baked cookies, helped with homework, and punished us when we were doing naughty things like I saw on TV. I wanted a daddy to tell me I was a pretty girl, give me a hug, and show real love without touching my privates. I wanted a grandma and grandpa who rocked in chairs on the porch, made lemonade in the summer, and told us old stories. I wanted to laugh with my brothers and get excited with them over birthday parties and Christmas presents. Were those things even real?

For a long time, it was just Mommy and my brothers. The morning Mommy got up and demanded we wash up, I knew she was up to something strange. She put us in matching, clean clothes. Our hair was combed; we had decent shoes on. We had to be going somewhere special because I had never seen us look so put together.

We pulled up to a pretty house with a large porch and manicured green lawn. There was no graffiti from the local gangs, no garbage on the streets. It looked like a house out of a book or magazine. Once inside, the interior matched the exterior.

The decor was shiny, placed, untouched. There were place mats on the table and hand towels in the bathroom. Everything matched and smelled so fresh. I immediately noticed the people in the room.

There was an older couple, hair graying and fine lines in their faces. In the background, I noticed two young girls. They were a little older than me. They had fair skin, blond-like hair, and light eyes. Compared to my brothers and me, they were completely different. They had on different gorgeous dresses. They had lace on their socks, and their shoes were so shiny and loud. They laughed and played as

I stared in confusion. Mommy looked at us and said, "Say hi to your grandma, grandpa, and sisters." My world spun. I felt dizzy, foggy, and hot. This startling news shook me. I have sisters? For so long, I was the only girl with two rough, dirty boys. How could I have sisters that I never knew? By the time it sank into my brain who these girls were, the lady whom Mommy said was Grandma started arguing with Mommy. Mommy quickly gathered my brothers and me and demanded it was time to go.

Soon after this brief introduction to my long-lost family, my new sisters came to our house to visit. When they entered into our door, their faces immediately cringed at the sights and smells. The difference between environments was shocking. The humiliation I felt for how my home looked was immense. Mommy didn't mind, but she never acknowledged a mess. I tried to talk to them, to find out about them, but they did not want to be bothered with me. They made fun of my brothers and me and our unsightly home. They did not like the food we ate or the neighborhood we lived in. They constantly ridiculed every aspect of our lives and compared them to how much better they had.

They made me feel more ashamed of where I was from. I no longer had the desire to get to know them because they never made any effort to even acknowledge me. One weekend, when they were supposed to visit, my brothers and I were outside. A beautiful, shiny big white car pulled up, and my sisters jumped out with large grins on their faces. My brothers and I looked up from the dirt pile we played in and gazed at the man who was driving. He reached into his pocket and pulled out his wallet. He gave my sisters some dollars. He then glanced at us, and he dug in his pocket again and reached for some change. He then flipped my brothers and me a couple of coins. We gathered the money and angrily marched into the house. We ran to Mommy and demanded she tell us who this man was. She snapped that he was our sisters' daddy. My mind rocked. They have a daddy? Where is our daddy? Why do we have different daddies? She revealed that Sam and I had a daddy and knew about us but didn't want us. He had a wife and a real family. She didn't mention Redd's daddy. I wanted more answers, but Mommy dismissed me.

This divide made me come to the realization of just how different we all looked. Sam and I both had dark hair and brown eyes and darker-toned skin. Redd had red hair and brighter eyes. My absent sisters were even lighter. The inequality was evident. Sam and I weren't allowed to go by our sisters' house, and Redd was allowed sometimes. I only saw my grandma a couple of times, and both times she made me feel cast out. The differences were apparent. My brothers and I never celebrated holidays—no birthdays, no Christmas. We did not have a TV for a long time. The toys and clothes we had were never new; they were already used and damaged and discarded. I recognized how unfair this was. It boiled me how we were treated differently. I did not understand why our daddies didn't want us and our sisters' daddy wanted them. What made us so bad? If Daddy didn't love me and Mommy didn't love me, how could a God love me?

This made me adamant that when I have my babies, they are going to all have the same daddy. My prepubescent mind was made up. I did not even understand how babies were made, but I knew that mine had to come from one man. The thought of my own children being divided and treated differently because they looked different disgusted me. It haunted me. I did not want my own kids looking at me and questioning me the way we did to Mommy. I would be a good mommy. I would have babies that loved me, appreciated me, and needed me. I wanted to feel that love.

One of the only times I saw Mommy cry was when she dropped the phone after being told my grandmother had died. Mommy demanded that we attend her funeral. I couldn't understand the purpose of funerals. Sue's dead body haunted my dreams for a long time; now I have another corpse to add to the nightmares. I did not want to say goodbye to this lady. This mean old lady, who in the couple of times I saw her, screamed at Mommy and disregarded us dirty, dark-looking children. As much as I fought, Mommy insisted. We were dressed in what we had as the best and were at the funeral home. Staring at her dead body made my skin crawl. I went to the back of the room, the farthest I could get from her casket. When people lined up to view her body, Mommy's sister violently grabbed my arm to take me with her. I cried and begged not to go close, but this fell upon her deaf ears. She demanded that I say goodbye to my grandma for the last time. I did not want to come close to her for fear that, since she hated me so much, she would especially haunt me. I swallowed the fear that engulfed me and stood by Mommy's side as I stared at this stiff old face. I gazed, wondering why she hated Mommy. I gazed at Mommy and wondered why she hated me. Why had this curse of loathing been passed down? How had it made it so far? I gazed and promised myself to love my babies.

By the time I was ten, I've lived a lifetime. I was happy that Butch was out of my life, and I only went by Bob's house when I had the need to get high. My two absent sisters came around more often. By this time, my oldest sister, Cindy, who was eighteen, had her own place. My other sister, Shannon, and her boyfriend, Brian, moved in with us because she was pregnant. I was so excited for Shannon. We were never close, but the thought of me being an auntie filled me with so much joy. I thrived at the thought of an innocent baby.

Most of my time was spent in the streets; school was an afterthought. I became my brothers' keeper. They recognized the beast within me that was created with the help of Butch. I did not mind fighting; I felt accomplished. I had an anger in me from all the pain I felt, and it had to escape. If it escaped on the boys and girls that messed with my brothers, I felt helpful. I became one of the boys. Doing girly things like experimenting with clothes and makeup did not interest me. I loved playing in dirt, tackling in football, and catching fish. My environment was filled with random boys.

One of these boys looked a lot like my brother Sam. He had tanned skin, curly thick dark hair, and the same-colored eyes. He would come over to play sometimes, but he blended in with the revolving door of kid, so I never gave it a thought. His name was Ernie. There was a time when his mommy took me, Sam, and Ernie to the local bar and let us pick out snacks. I noticed the man behind the bar. He was large, and he had the same curly thick hair and dark eyes. He didn't say anything, but he whispered to Ernie's mom and glared at us. There was something about this man. I felt that I recognized him but had never seen him before. Was this even possible? He was so familiar; his face haunted me, and I could not let it go.

Whenever I saw Ernie, his mom would take both Sam and me and go by her house to spend time and play. This confused me. I was anticipating something happening, and it began to bother me that it didn't. The fact that I saw this stranger once and could not stop thinking about him bothered me. I finally got enough courage to ask Ernie who this man was that was working in the bar. He looked at me dumbfounded and confused. He replied, "He's our daddy."

"Our daddy?" What did he mean "our daddy"? Ernie explained that he was my and Sam's brother and that man was our father. I felt like I was going to faint. This did not seem real. I felt that at any moment, I was going to wake up. I was bewildered by the fact that I actually had a daddy and confused that I had another brother. No one told me. How could they know all this time and not inform me? The man I always wondered about stared me in the face and never said a word. I had a slew of questions that no one had an answer for. I could not understand why he never saw us; he knew who we were and never said anything. How could he leave us with Mommy? We lived in filth, we were hungry, and monsters were after me. He could have saved me. He could have taken me away from the pain and fear. I hated him. He just rejected me and Sam and created a whole new family.

What made Ernie better than me? Did I have other brothers and sisters? Could they possibly rescue us? I was again rejected and cast off to fend for myself. Once I found this out, we moved away. We would eventually move back to the same neighborhood, but I would never see my dad again, and I stopped seeing Ernie. I would write letters to my dad and try to give them to Mommy to deliver, and she would snap that he was married and didn't want us. I soon stopped trying. I was never more alone. I came to the conclusion that Daddy was never coming for me.

Mommy's attempt at being a wife and better mother came when she married Jim. I didn't meet him until after they were married and he moved in. She took off on us for a weekend, and by Sunday, Jim was her husband and living with us. Mommy didn't act the same. Our house was clean; I had never seen it so clean. The piles were gone, the stench was no longer lingering, and we had food to eat.

She even cooked dinner. Jim was mean. He hated us. He deliberately made life hell; he especially hated me. He would urinate in my closet, lock the refrigerator, and give me things only to take them back days later. We were not his kids, so he despised us. He would drink every day and become extremely violent. The day he came home after an arm injury and had a cast on, I took my revenge. I saw he was weakened, and I was fed up. I began to fight back. I threw an ashtray when he broke the glass door and it cut my mother. When he chased me, I picked up a heavy piece of wood and smashed his recovering arm as hard as I could. It gave me pleasure to see him in pain. Eventually, he bowed out and left. He moved to Oregon and tried his best to get Mommy to get rid of me, take the boys, and run off. She never did, which surprised me. I really never understood why she did not leave. I was afraid she would. She did not care what happened to me, so what would she stay for?

Love

In church, the preacher talked a lot about love, how God loves us and we should love one another. I had no idea what that entailed. Is love the touching between my legs? But love is supposed to be a good feeling, a comforting feeling, and those touches were not good or comforting. Those feelings were ugly, sickening. Mommy doesn't say she loves me. No one says they love me. Love was an abstract idea. I knew it was out there somewhere, but I could not see it or feel it. I so badly wanted it. I wanted to be able to give it. I cared, but I did not know what it meant to love.

As time went on and I got a bit older, I was desperate for love. I continued to go by Bob's house for his party favors. I felt a lot older than the other kids in my neighborhood; my torture aged me. I felt I was ready for something bigger. This is when I met Barry. I knew Barry and his family from running around the neighborhood. It did not take long for me to like Barry, and we became boyfriend and girlfriend. Sex was not a big deal to me. Men took what they wanted from me, so now it was up to me as to whom I gave myself to. I felt like I loved Barry, and the thought of a baby took me over. I desired love, and I wanted it however and from whomever I could get it. I loved babies. I babysat every chance I got. Many times, I babysat for the local prostitutes while they worked. I knew that those babies probably didn't have all that great of a mommy just like me. I wanted to show them love that they probably weren't getting. My need for my own baby overtook me. Having my own baby made me think nothing but love.

At the same time I met Barry, I met who would become my best friend, Laura. Laura and I were inseparable. She was the only girl I ever met who was not stuck-up. She was extremely relatable, and she lived next door. Whenever you saw one of us, the other was not far behind. She was the one who taught me about my period. I did not know about sex or my period from anyone except her. Laura loves me like a sister. She had a huge family with lots of sisters, but they seemed so cold toward one another. We talked about things that she could never talk to her sisters about. I could never talk to my sisters; I barely knew them. And talking to my brothers about girl stuff was out of the question. We did everything together, and I finally had someone I could confide in and trust.

Laura had an older brother, Andy. He was way older than me, but I seemed so much older to everyone that they did not notice my age. As Laura and I became close, Andy took every opportunity to hit on me. He wanted to be with me, but I was with Barry at that time. Barry was extremely sweet and well-mannered, but Andy was a drug dealer. He had weed and money. He was always doing things; he had a car. It wasn't long before I gave in to Andy's advances and broke up with Barry. I felt bad, but Andy offered an escape; he offered security. These were the things I needed; these were things I never had. I desperately wanted a family, and a baby required that I had money. I did not want to be like my mommy. I wanted my baby fed, clean, and in a house of our own. I cared about Andy. I said I loved him, but I loved what he offered more. Andy was a lot older than me, but having sex with him didn't bother me. I was used to older men using me up, so being with another one did not matter to me; what mattered was that it was by my choice. I felt that I needed to take back power over my life, and whether it was having sex, having a baby, or getting high, it was done because I wanted to do it.

Very soon after being with Andy, my period stopped. From my talks with Laura, I knew that this was a sign I was pregnant. When I went to the clinic and it was confirmed, my insides melted with ecstasy. I finally had a purpose; I was going to be a mommy. I would be a good mommy. I would love my baby, and my baby would return my love. Once Jim left Mommy, her house went back to the disgusting sty it was before. I could not bring my baby home to this. Andy and I got our own place, and I took pride in my house.

We did not have a lot of money, but we had money. Andy was a popular drug dealer, and money was steady coming in. I cleaned our home every day and cooked meals. It was just a room in a crowded building, but it was ours. I was able to escape Bob, the other drug dealers, the local prostitutes, and the violence. I was safe in my own clean environment. I was in bliss. I still smoked weed when I wanted, but no one was going to tell me what to do. Andy was not the warmest man, but he gave me what I wanted, and he was happy that I was having his baby. I was happy that I was closer to Laura. We were now family; she was going to be my baby's auntie. She cried with excitement when I told her the news. We looked forward to this breath of fresh air that was living inside of me. I was filled with love and the happiest I had been my entire life.

Reality

Andy was not the warmest man. Our conversations were surface conversations. He did not talk about feelings or dreams of the future. He was not really affectionate, but I saw him as stable, and stability was something that I never had yet needed now that I was pregnant. Andy demanded control. The task of cooking and cleaning was something that I wanted to do, but soon it became something required of me. He was increasingly controlling, but my young mind wanted that structure, so I did not see it as a problem. The problem came when I surprised him by coming home earlier than he thought. The problem came when I saw him facedown and snorting a line of cocaine. My mind spun with outrage and confusion. I angrily yelled and screamed, "What the fuck are you doing?" I could not believe he was doing coke. We all smoked weed, but we knew better than to be strung out on dope! Andy immediately stood up, backed his heavy hand, and whipped it across my face. The force stung my face and pushed me back into a dresser. As my pregnant body slid down to the floor, he scolded me about questioning him. I was thirteen years old, six months pregnant and was just hit by the twenty-year-old father of my baby. I was in shock. I could not believe he could hit me with his baby inside of me. My heart shattered; my hopes of control diminished immediately. I was stuck. I wanted my baby more than anything in the world, and I could not rob my baby of its father.

My baby had to have a daddy. I desperately kept my mouth closed, got up, and gathered my tears. I left him alone in the room to finish what he began, and I was left alone to cope with what I had entered into.

I did not know what to do; I had nowhere to go. My only hope had a heartbeat inside of me, and I knew I had to keep it safe. I had to bear whatever Andy gave me. There was a greater purpose now. My baby had to have a daddy, even if he was foul. The fighting and smacks became a routine. I walked on eggshells as any random thing would set him off, but I would not allow him to hurt our baby like he hurt me. I was devoted to doing everything within my power to keep my baby safe. This included moving out of the room we were living in and escaping some of the drug deals that happened down the hallway. I hated having to move back in with Mommy. Her house was disgusting and no place for my baby. I knew this was temporary until we got a better place, but it made me sick just being there.

The moment my baby girl was born, I finally knew what true love felt like. That was the moment that I was able to love and felt the love in return. Not my grandma, not my mommy, not Andy—no one had ever shown me what love was. My baby, my perfect, pure baby, was filled with love. I spent hours just staring at her, and all the evils of the world melted and faded away in those moments.

Showing my baby to everyone we knew, including Laura, brought so much joy to me. Laura was ecstatic to have a niece. We would take walks while Andy was at work and continue to sell weed. Laura and I would spend hours just talking, laughing, and confiding all our problems to each other. It bothered me when Cindy got Shannon and her son out of Mommy's house because of how sickening it was. No one cared about me and my baby. I was determined to do what I had to do on my own to get out.

Cope

Coping is a skill that does not come easy. Usually, it is mastered under extreme stress and traumatic experiences. The outlet used is not always healthy. Before I was pregnant, I used alcohol. Now that there was life inside of me, my only outlet was marijuana. I would still leave my body. Anytime I was in a situation that required too much of me, I could not handle it. I escaped my mind, retreated from my own body. Soon those experiences, those memories became foggy. I needed this fog. I needed a blanket to hide me from them, keep me warm and safe. If they can't see me, they can't attack me.

Throughout my life, I had no choice but to cope: cope with the neglect, cope with the molestation, cope with the rape, and cope with the beatings. I came to the realization very quickly that I had no one to save me. My only way of coping was talking to Laura. She understood me so well. I always thought being soul mates was a bond shared between a man and a woman who were in a relationship, but Laura and I were soul mates for sure. We knew what the other was thinking just by looking at each other's faces. We did everything together.

My only outlet of cope was, unfortunately, cut short. When my baby was three months old, Laura invited me to go out with her and her sisters to have fun. I desperately wanted to escape the house and do something different. Andy was not giving in. My baby was colicky from being sick, and he did not want to take care of her, so I was stuck at home. Unbeknownst to me, that night, while Laura's inebriated older sister got behind the wheel, she lost control of the car. The car crashed head-on into a pole on a bridge. I got a call that there was an accident, but no one would tell me about Laura. It was not until I watched the news where they reported one victim dead. As the body lay on the stretcher with a blanket covering it, I knew by the shoes she was wearing that this was my Laura. Those were her favorite shoes. I was supposed to go with her; I was supposed to die with her, with my best friend. She left me in this world alone to fend for myself. I had no one.

My world crashed. Everything was bland, white, and distant. People paused, sound stopped, I dropped to the floor and hysterically yelped out helpless screams. She was the only one I ever fully trusted. Even worse, she was so incredibly excited to be pregnant. We were going to raise our babies together. We were going to grow up together. No one ever could take her place, and as much as I tried to find another friend as loyal and kind as her, I never could. I never got over her death; I carry her with me every day. I learn to cope every day without her by numbing. The pain of missing her never goes away, and it deflated me from ever having a true friendship like ours again. She was my sister, and she was gone.

I was haunted by her memory for a long time. I had continuous nightmares that included visions of Laura coming to me and telling me that I need to come with her. She would beg me to leave with her, to not leave her alone. It made my soul ache. As my baby daughter, Rachel, continued to grow up, her face was so familiar. Her features favored Laura's so much; my daughter was God's token. She was my daily reminder of my best friend.

Coping with my world got harder. The arguments with Andy got worse. His drug use got heavier. My need for numbness got stronger, and the beatings got horrific. I continued to be too embarrassed to go anywhere because of black eyes and swollen lips. I entertained going back to school, but that thought faded when I realized that I'd have to meet people and that those people would be looking at me, judging me. I rarely left the house.

I became so incredibly sad. My sadness was not a cry and "get over it" sad. My sad was a rock, a huge boulder that I was forced to carry around with me everywhere I went. I felt like people could see it, and they were constantly whispering, asking "What's wrong with her?" The rock weighed me down, took my energy. The rock became a sickness, an emptiness, and I tried to fill it with everything. I found that slicing my skin with razors or knives would drain me of the sickness. The cold pain would remind me I was still alive yet punish me. This became a disturbingly comfortable ritual. I have learned to numb myself so well that I crave to feel. Sinking a razor into my flesh makes me feel the pain.

Eventually, Andy and I moved out of my mommy's disgusting house and got a small one-bedroom apartment. It was not much, but it was mine. It felt amazing to leave her and be on my own. I would get her to watch Rachel on the weekends, and Andy and I would party hard. The drinking, weed smoking, acid dropping, coke snorting, and pill popping would put me in a cloud so high that I did not care about the punches that were thrown at my face or the chairs being broken over my back.

It made me not care that I was with a man who hated me. I would have to clean up and clear the fog before being back in "mommy mode." It was the only way to cope with my environment. I couldn't get away from Laura's death or Butch's touches because they haunted my dreams constantly.

It was not long before Andy's treatment took its toll on me. The names he called me, the threats, and the beatings took any infatuation I had toward him and demolished it. I began to take interest in other boys. I met Freddy, who was one of Andy's friends and a fellow drug dealer. As I was being more and more mistreated, I drew closer to Freddy. I confided my problems in him, and he would say the sweetest things to make me feel better. He would tell jokes, be funny, and make me laugh so hard.

Andy was never this way with me anymore. I had to tiptoe around Andy. I had to keep a clean house and hot meals. There was no down time or relaxing with Andy. Freddy gave me an outlet to be free with a man. I felt free—mind, body, and soul—while I was with him. Drugs were used to enhance us, not to keep me from feeling him. His words were sweeter, and his touch was smoother. I felt love. It was different from the love I thought I had with Andy, so it had to be real.

I continued to be the homemaker I was. I cleaned and cooked every day and catered to my baby girl the best I knew how. I would continue to party on the weekend with Andy but carry on with my love affair with Freddy. I felt like I was three different people in one, and I got a thrill from it. Being around both Andy and Freddy at the same time made me slightly nervous at first, but it wasn't too long before I got a thrill from it. I was secretly satisfied that I was cheating on Andy. I had no doubts that he did what he wanted when he left that door, so it was only right that I had my own life as well.

Soon Andy made us move from our small apartment. He got increasingly paranoid about selling drugs from a large apartment building. Neighbors would complain about foot traffic or the loud noises from our fights. Andy made us live with his mom to save some money. I had no choice but to go with. Unfortunately, our living corners would be in Laura's old bedroom. This triggered horrific nightmares about Laura for a long time. I was deprived of peace. Whatever relaxation I thought I could get, sleep was stolen from me by haunting visions of Laura. Now as an adult, I realize that they weren't just nightmares; they were night terrors, visions of Laura so real that I felt I could reach out and hug her. Her constant pleading for me to come with her made my heart cry for her. I wanted to be with her so bad. I wanted her to be the best aunt to my kids like I knew she would be. I wanted to be there for her when she had her baby. There was so much she was missing and so much that I wanted to tell her. I would bolt out of these visions in sweat, with tears streaming from my eyes and my heart speeding.

Andy was never there for me. His position was about money. He made sure he had money coming into the home, but there was no emotional connection whatsoever. He was cold all the time. There was no consoling, no affection, and no opinions. I was not in a relationship. I was under a dictatorship. What he said went, and if I even cracked my lips to say anything different, I was on the receiving end of his wrath. I was hopeful that moving into the home of Andy's mother would keep him from beating me. But this made no difference to him. We would still scream, and he would hit me relentlessly. His mom would overhear our fighting and tell me to just be quiet and listen to what he said so that I didn't make him hit me. During this time, I began to get closer to Andy's other sisters, Tina and Lena, but neither one could replicate the bond that I lost with Laura.

Startling Surprise

All this time, Freddy and I carried on our affair. He had a girlfriend, and I had Andy, but neither one of us were happy with them. We connected on a deeper level. It was amazing to let my guard down and fall in love with someone who adored me in return. We were having sex regularly, and it was because I wanted to. It was not too long after my daughter's first birthday that I found out I was pregnant again. I was ecstatic. The only problem was that I was not sure who the father was. I prayed and hoped it was Freddy, but I knew that there was a probability that it could also be Andy's. I did not want to be Mommy. She had five kids and three different daddies. I did not want my babies to grow up like me, having different daddies and being treated unfairly. Not too much later, Freddy told me that his girlfriend was pregnant, and my heart ripped in two. He was raised to do the right thing, and he married his girlfriend. I knew he married her because she got pregnant. The night he got married, he spent the night with me. This cemented the fact that his wife did not mean anything to him and his heart was really with me.

I told Andy that the baby was his, but I told Freddy the truth. He wished I told him earlier. He was extremely excited that I might be carrying his baby. Money was a great motivator. I was sixteen when my son was born, and I was at odds. A huge part of me wanted my baby to be Freddy's, but I so badly wanted a stable life, and part of stability meant that both my kids would be from one man. Andy was a horrible person, but he provided financially for me and my daughter, so I knew he would continue to at least do that. I desperately wanted to escape his hateful wrath and his violence and live happily ever after with Freddy, but I didn't know what that would mean for my kids.

I gave birth to a beautiful baby boy right after my daughter turned two. I named him after Andy, and this made the guilt I was feeling even stronger. Freddy and I decided it was the smartest thing to come clean and get a paternity test. Freddy and I sat down with Freddy's wife and Andy and told them the truth. To say they were angry would be putting it nicely. I already knew what I had coming from Andy. He would never let this go. It did not take long for our court date to arrive and to find out the results of the testing. My mind and heart were on two different roads. My mind wanted Andy to be the father. It made logical sense to my immature mind. I wanted my babies to have the same daddy. I did not want them to be treated differently. Even if their daddy was a monster, at least they would know who he was. There would be no guessing, no wondering; no investigation needed to be done. My heart wanted Freddy. I was so in love with this man. Even though he was married to someone else, I knew he was in love with me. I had a connection with him that never existed with Andy, and I knew he would be a great father to my baby. Ultimately, my mind won the race. My son was Andy's baby. After this shock to my heart, mommy mode was in full effect. It hurt me so bad when I had to tell Freddy that not only our affair but also our friendship had to be over. It was for the sake of my kids; I had to pretend to love Andy. I desperately wanted my family to stay together. No matter the names I was called or how badly I was beaten, I was desperate for normalcy.

Growing Pains

By the time I was sixteen, I had two kids, and I was ecstatic to finally be able to get emancipated. I demanded my mommy sign the papers. I was an adult with my own family, and I needed to apply for assistance to ensure that my babies were taken care of. She did not put up a fight. I was hoping that I would receive enough welfare to maybe escape Andy's control and be on my own once my kids were old enough. Welfare was a slap in the face. The assistance helped, but it was nowhere near enough to support us. I needed Andy's money to make sure my kids had a roof over their heads and food in their mouths.

The beatings continued. I was eighteen, and my kids were four and two years old. I began to fight Andy back when he would not stop hitting me, but this made him even angrier and the beatings worse. I was completely numb—mind, body, and soul. Andy would yell at our kids when they did something wrong, but I refused to let him lay a hand on them. I was the disciplinarian. The thought of him trying to spank them terrified me. I knew he would lose control and hurt them worse than intended.

Andy got a job that required him to work third shift. Those were my hours of freedom. Whenever I got the chance to get a babysitter, I partied into oblivion. I easily got a fake ID and went to the bars whenever I could. I binged on alcohol to forget all the pain that lay behind my eyes. I would go to bars a lot with Andy's sisters to keep a witness with me in case he accused me of cheating on him. He was incredibly insecure. This only worked a minority of the time. He would still come up with paranoid excuses for hitting me. Our relationship was tremulous, to say the least. I would endure his abuse, then he would try to make it up to me. He proposed marriage more than once, but I declined. I had a long-term plan in mind.

I knew I would leave him eventually. When my kids were old enough to remember him and know him, I would save us from him.

This lifestyle and the things I saw were nothing compared to the things that were done to me since I was a child. Nothing mattered to me but my kids. I lost Freddy, and he was the only man I have known to love me. I did not care what happened to me. I had an emptiness in my heart that, as much as I tried to fill it with stuff, was still bare. Not the drugs, the alcohol, men—nothing could fill it. It caused a sore, a hole inside me that made me cut everyone off if they got too close, even my own kids. I showed them love, but if they became too clingy or emotional, it made me incredibly uncomfortable. I never was shown this affection, so it was a difficult concept for me to grasp and give to anyone else. I've been punished over and over for things I never did, so why not do them and have the fun I could if I was going to receive punishment for it anyway?

This was my mentality when I met Raulph. After bars would close, a bunch of us would go to someone's house to continue our after-hours party. I recognized him at one of these parties. I used to babysit for his sister, and I knew he was a boxer, but he got into trouble and was in and out of jail repeatedly. We talked, and our conversation flowed so naturally. I liked him. He knew I was with Andy, but that didn't stop him from wanting to set up a date. I agreed. He was really genuine and was honest about all the trouble he got into. We both talked to each other about our dreams for the future and what we hoped to gain out of life. These hopes and dreams were nice to talk to someone about, but I doubted that they would ever come true. All my dreams and hopes were snatched away from me early on by monsters. I had no idea how to get them back. If it meant facing those monsters again, I gave up.

I spent my time taking care of my kids, my home, putting up with Andy, and meeting up with Raulph. There was a night when Andy and I got into a huge fight, and after I fought back by kicking him as hard as I could in the balls, he picked up a heavy wooden chair and broke it over my back and head. I went black. I passed out cold and slid onto the floor. Andy's little sister screamed and thought I had died. As I slowly awoke, M called the police, and they came to make sure I was okay. They tried their hardest to pursue me to proceed with charges against Andy. I made a deal with him. I wouldn't follow up with charges if he agreed to leave me alone, and of course, he agreed.

Over the next few weeks, I felt great. It was amazing not walking on eggshells, not being questioned for every word that came out of my mouth for fear of being a punching bag. Andy would call and harass me, pleading me to come back, but I stood my ground. I continued a blossoming relationship with Raulph. I finally felt like I was moving forward. I finally felt like I was becoming strong—a stronger mom, a stronger woman.

Life

Life has a strange way of smacking you in the face with your own irony. My life has been an example of this. While everyone around me was skating by when doing wrong, I was punished immediately for every one of my wrongdoings. There was no hiding my face. I was punished relentlessly by God. This created a bitterness in me. Just as I felt when Andy would punish me when I did nothing wrong, I felt the same way when bad things in my life would occur that I had no explanation for. I felt that God was punishing me for things that I didn't do. I did not understand how God is supposed to be loving yet does nothing to the monsters who violated me as a child. Where was God when Andy was balling up his fists and pounding me into sleep?

Life kicked me, beat me, called me horrific names, and then held me in its arms and told me that it would never happen again. I believed it. Through every hellish nightmare I have been through, there's something deep under all that rot that tells me to hang on. Through my screaming and the tears streaming down my face, there's a soft voice. Through all the gallons of alcohol, the marijuana smoke, and the cocaine dust, there's a hopeful heart. Were there times of fear? No doubt. Did I lose hope at times and want to end my life? Absolutely. Somehow even in these desperate times, that nagging voice would grow louder, and that hopeful heart would pound harder.

God has been an overall presence in my life. Every time I had an internal dialogue, I was speaking to Him, pleading to Him, thanking Him, and questioning Him. Slowly I understand why He has allowed certain things to evolve in my life, but I know that I won't ever find out most of it. Often things from my past, mistakes, and people have a way of making a full circle in my life so that I run into them again. I have come to take this as a great lesson. I am stubborn and hardheaded. I have been alone all my life. I never had anyone to defend me or fight for my survival. If I wanted to live, I had to fight for myself. Often if things would not work the way I wanted them to, I would try to find a way to make it work. These things were not always good, and those were the things that would backfire.

It seemed as if God was not going to let me get away with anything. My friends would steal, sell drugs, and hustle in many other ways. That life was intriguing to me and seemed the only way to make a living, but it never failed that my dishonesty and maleficence would always catch up with me while others would get away clean. One would think that I would learn my lesson early on and realize that God was trying to tell me something. But while God knocked on the door to my heart, I kept ignoring it and listening to the devil telling me that I could get away with it.

Since my innocent childhood was ripped away from me early on, I spent a lot of my life reliving it. I yearned for love and attention. The awkward stares of strangers would terrify me. But while drunk or high, I was on top of the world, the life of the party. Dancing, laughing, telling jokes, and conversing were comfortable when I had the anesthetic of substances rushing in my blood. It seemed I was my better self. I was outgoing, smarter, prettier, and sexier when I had the confidence that came with partying.

The devil has a way of creeping in and providing things to you in your time of desperation. The concept of God was so confusing to me. Watching people in church, including my own mother, being such hypocrites made me disregard what God wanted for me. Doing bad was easier; ignoring God was easier. Trying to figure out what God was all about was perplexing to me. It was an overwhelming task. It stayed behind the scenes in my heart, and no matter how I tried to drown out those concepts, those feelings never released. That need for God, that hunger for His Word and love stayed.

Tragedy over Triumph

I was beginning to get used to being on my own. I continued to grow with Raulph and take care of my kids, and my life was finally feeling like it was in bloom. I began to revisit all the things I had wanted to do for so long but Andy would stop. I thought about going back to school and making something of myself. I was not sure what I wanted to work as, but I knew I could do something that had more purpose. I hated meeting new people. Being confronted with judgmental, interrogational questions raised a panic inside my heart. It would make my mind race, my skin crawl, and my eyes would search for the quickest way out. But as long as I did not have to hide bruises on top of this feeling, I actually thought it could be conquered. I was realizing my dreams and exploring hope. I think I was in one of these dreams while walking to a friend's house with my two babies when I heard the screeching sounds of tires on the pavement. As I looked behind me, I saw evil. I saw the dark, wild eyes glaring at me, and they belonged to Andy. His brows furrowed, and his teeth gnashed while he stopped the car on the sidewalk in front of me and blocked my path.

My heart sank to my toes. I felt nauseated and knew that darkness was coming. As he jumped out of the car, "bitches," "sluts," and "hoes" were the words I heard in between others. He began with the smacks, smacking me in the back of the head and sides of my face so hard that it throbbed my entire head. Explicit names streamed from his mouth as he pushed me along the sidewalk. My mind rang; I was filled with terror, dread, shock, and anxiety. I yelled and screamed to the passersby to help me. Was he going to kill me right on a public street? What about my kids? They would see their mother die. Why were people just staring at us? Why wasn't anyone calling the police?

I sped up my walk, trying to discreetly get away from him, but his abuse was relentless. I then saw a truck drive a little past us and pull over at the side of the road. I saw a familiar man leap out the cabin and, after a few seconds, realized it was Raulph! He ran up to us and began yelling "I see what you are doing, punk! Be a man and fight me instead!" They began to fight, and Raulph's boxing past began to show. The smacking sounds of Raulph's fists hitting Andy in the face were a delight to my ears. It was a relieving feeling to see Andy finally get back all the beating he dealt to me. I relished in it; I bathed in the sight and got gleeful at the thought of him in pain.

After Raulph thought Andy had enough, he escorted me away. Raulph began staying with me to protect me from Andy's retaliation. I was extremely appreciative, and this only made Raulph and me grow closer. While Raulph was at work, Andy would still call me and threaten me daily. I thought it was all talk, but every time I was alone, I was constantly checking locks and looking over my shoulder. Andy was not around, but I could not help but walk on eggshells anyway. Even when he was not physically abusing me, he haunted my mentality. Still, I had no peace.

One night, Raulph and I decided we were going to go out, so I got a babysitter for my kids. We went out to the bars, met up with mutual friends, had drinks and a great time. We went back home to unwind, and as we were relaxing, we heard loud banging on the door. Quickly and with strength, the door rattled until a loud crack occurred, with Andy breaking through to finish what was started on the street. Raulph leaped up and grabbed a sawed-off shotgun he had stashed in the bedroom and raised it toward Andy. He pleaded with Andy to leave because he did not want to have to shoot him. Watching Raulph's intense face and Andy glaring back was beyond intense. As much as I hated Andy, I did not want the father of my children to die. I jumped in front of the gun and turned to Andy, demanding him to leave. Andy followed our demands and stormed out.

We were relieved but still did not feel safe, so we packed up and left the house, deciding to stay at a friend's for the night. We got a few blocks down the street when I heard the familiar screams of the tires again. This time, Andy didn't stop on the side of us; he was behind us and threatening to run us over. He eventually pulled over and got out of the car, and he was holding a thick metal pole. As soon as Raulph saw him get out, he retrieved the shotgun again from the duffel bag he was carrying. Andy ran toward Raulph with the pole, and Raulph didn't hesitate to pull back on the trigger and let out a sparkling blast from the riffle.

The explosion hit Andy in the abdomen, and he immediately doubled over onto the ground. In the blink of an eye, there was a hole in this man's stomach, and the blood gushing out of his wound puddled around him. In my adrenaline-fueled mind, I ran. I am not sure where Raulph ran off to after he pulled his trigger, but I ran to my older sister's house. As I banged on the door and it was opened, my body filled with sickness, and I vomited. My face was hot and sticky, and my body was trembling. I did not know how to process the scene. Was Andy dead? Was the father of my kids dead in the street? Was I going to jail? My kids would have no one to raise them. Tears streamed down my face in regret. I hated him, but I would have never wanted him to die. I caused this. Once again, it was my fault. Once again, I was punished. I heard sirens but could not move. I was told that Andy was taken by ambulance. I found out what hospital he was and found out that he made it through surgery.

Raulph was found by police. Once he told the story and I told what happened, the situation was deemed self-defense. Unfortunately, Raulph was on probation when this happened, so he had to serve time. Andy's entire intestines were damaged, and it would take multiple surgeries and a long recovery before he was healed. With Andy in the hospital and Raulph in jail again, I had no other means of money. My kids and I were completely struggling. I did everything I could just to keep food in the house. I donated my blood for money twice a week and sold drugs when I could.

Once Andy was able to, he began calling me from the hospital. His phone calls were filled with crying, begging, and blaming me for what happened to him.

I was vulnerable, and he knew it. He saw the good that was deep down in me, and he used it to his advantage. He knew that despite how much I hated him, I could not stand by and watch anyone suffer if I could do something to help. He guilted me every single chance he got. He knew I had no money and was despairing about how I was going to take care of the kids. I was worried, I was alone, and I was incredibly ashamed of my part in what happened to Andy. I was responsible for my kids, and I was responsible for what happened to Andy, so I caved. I agreed to let Andy back in once he was released from the hospital. I felt it was my fault that he was there, so it was my job to help him get better. Had I not had kids by him, I am sure I would have been done with him a long time ago.

I had to do everything I could to offer my children a life of normalcy. I knew the life they were born in was not normal, but compared to the life I was born in, it was going to be better—that is, all I wanted for them was better. I wanted them to know that they had both a mother and a father. I wanted them to never know the feeling of being dirty, of being hungry and cold. I wanted them to be protected even if it was just me doing it. I was going to do it till it killed me. I wanted them to think everything was okay even though at times they could not be worse. I had seen bad mommy after bad mommy. I did what I could to be a good mommy. I wanted my babies to grow to be happy and healthy.

Although my relationship with God was tremulous, to say the least, I still prayed. I prayed that my kids would learn from the mistakes I had made and will continue to make for a long time. Despite the rumors of so-called friends and family, my intentions are good. Given my circumstances, my lack of education, my mental illnesses, my insecurities and fears, I only want the best for the people I love.

Hard Decision

Andy was released from the hospital, and I took him in. Bandage changes, colostomy bags, doctor's appointments, medication schedules, helping him walk normally—I did it all. Then I had missed a period. I took a pregnancy test, and it was positive. While Andy was in the hospital and Raulph was in prison, I looked for comfort in another man. I knew this pregnancy was his doing. I was honest with Andy and told him I was pregnant by someone else. Andy was adamant that I get an abortion. He rubbed it in my face about the situation with Freddy and getting a paternity test for our son. Since the man I was seeing was black, the baby would not look like the rest of our kids, and Andy was not going to be embarrassed again.

I caved in to Andy's demands—not just for him, but once again to try to maintain my family, to try to maintain having one father for all my kids. It felt like the doctor slaughtered me and reached deep into my soul to take out the part that, to this day, I feel missing. It was violating, traumatizing; it seared my conscience and troubled my soul for as long as I live. My depression stomped me deeper there for the blade would go deeper into my skin. I used my power of numbing on that cold surgical table as they killed the life inside of me, so I deserved my punishment of gliding that blade over and over into my own flesh. I knew what I did was a sin, and I doubted that God loved me. I did not deserve His love. I was a horrible person. The devil had written it in my heart that I was a no-good shit of a mother and woman. The life of my baby was ripped out of me. Even though it was not Andy's baby, it was mine, and I desperately wanted it. Out of all the things Andy took from me—my hopes, dreams, dignity, this by far was the worst.

Andy gave his fists a break until he fully recovered from his shooting, but as soon as he was strong enough, the reckless, merciless beatings continued. We were back to the regularly scheduled program. He constantly brought up the past to remind me of what a horrible person I was. He would knock me unconscious on a regular basis, take chairs, tables, and other various furniture, and throw them at me and my back. I tried to fight back every time. I've stabbed him often. The time he punched me dead in my face and knocked me down the wall, I grabbed a knife I had in my sock and reached back and pushed the knife into his chest as hard as I could. This time, he didn't block my aim. He ran out the house and yelled in the street for help as I ran and hid at a friend's house. I was afraid of going to jail and being taken away from my babies. He went to the hospital, and the blade of the knife missed his heart by a quarter of an inch. Andy told the police that the stabbing was done by some random person on the street, not me. The story was in the local paper. I was relieved that I avoided charges, but in all honesty, I wished that blade went through his heart. I had such a strong hatred toward him that just looking at him made my skin crawl. I was so young when he caught me in his web; he preyed on my inexperience. I was naive that there was any hope for me without his financial support. I had no future, which means I could not provide a future for my babies. The fighting and violence continued. It was almost a daily occurrence. I knew that I was not in this forever. I just needed some financial stability and for my kids to be old enough to really know their father.

When I tell people what I went through with Andy, I get looks. I get the looks of people asking me, How stupid could I be? What made me stay for so long? My brain and heart were not mature. My brain lacked the knowledge of a proper education. My heart lacked love. He baited me, tricked me with what I thought was love but was really control. He defiled me and held me so tight in his abusive grasp that I was convinced I had no options, no way out. Even when I tried and succeeded to leave, to move on, it was always temporary. He manipulated me like a toy, like a puppet. He played my good heart against me. He knew that I could not stand to see anyone, even someone I despised, in pain or in need of help. God gave me a conscience, and as much as I did wrong despite it, Andy had a way of tapping into it for his benefit.

Never Ending

Year after year, I'd wake up to Andy's face and feel nauseated. By the time I was twenty years old, I decided that I wanted one last baby; I used Andy. I was insistent upon all my kids having the same biological father, and unfortunately, Andy was it. It was not long before I became pregnant. I gave birth to my third beautiful baby girl at twenty-one.

I knew that I was done having babies, especially because if I wanted more, it meant I had to endure more years of Andy. I decided to have a tubal ligation after my daughter was born.

Andy had no further use for me. I was done having his babies. I liked having the extra money, but it was not worth living in hell with a man that I was not in love with. After another fight, I finally broke it off with him. I looked deep within my spirit and prayed for the courage to stand up to him for myself and my kids. He moved out, but not without a fight and harassment. He assumed that this time was going to be like every other time and I would eventually cave in. It was extremely difficult. The only income I was receiving was my state assistance, but I struggled to make it work. Andy continued his stalking and threats. He broke my windows, flattened tires, and spread lies about me to friends. The numbness I have nourished for so long kicked in, and I was cold toward his advances. He could no longer hurt me. I threatened him with police and restraining orders. Over time, he gave up on his pursuit of me.

Unfortunately, he also gave up on pursuing his own children. He started off picking them up, taking them to the zoo and other places. These visits became more and more sporadic, and eventually, his promises to them became more and more unreliable before he just stopped communicating with them altogether. It would break my heart to watch them get excited to see him and spend time with their father only to watch their tears fall when he would never show up. I hated that they were experiencing this heartbreak. As much as I hated Andy, I refused to say anything negative about him to the kids; I did not have to. My goal of them being old enough to know him was reached. They saw with their own eyes and heard with their own ears how he treated me and how much of an unreliable, terrible father he became. His child support was uneventful. Every time he would get a job, and by the time the state tracked him down to garnish his wages, he would quit and find something different.

I could not help but feel like a failure in my goal for my kids to have a good father. I knew that Andy was not a great man, but he provided financially for our kids. My kids were old enough to know who he was, but they also knew that he was a horrible person. They were around for the name-calling and the violence. They saw it so often that it became a common part of life for them, and for this, my heart ached. I wanted to change the dynamic, the curse of fatherlessness throughout my family. I honestly tried to give my kids an upstanding father in their lives but realized that I cannot force anyone to do what should be a responsibility to them.

As good as my intentions might have been for my children, unfortunately, they witnessed some extremely dark moments in my life.

In my goal for my kids to have a better life, as my son grew to be a preteen, he seemed to get into more and more trouble. He did not have a father figure in his life. Andy was a bad dad and soon became a nonexistent dad. My son started getting into fights, stealing and was constantly being harassed by gang members trying to recruit him. I had to make a move for him, a move that would break my heart. I decided to allow him to move to Missouri with my younger brother Sam. Sam was married with kids and was stable. I knew that he was the best option for my son to see what it meant to be a responsible, strong man. I could not teach him that as hard as I wanted to try. I ripped my heart, and a piece of it left with my baby boy as he left me. It made me feel incredibly guilty. I did not give up on my son, but this was for his benefit. I knew I was an addict and could not keep a stable environment for him and the problems he was facing.

Moving On

I finally decided to try to get some kind of education under my belt to possibly get a decent job. I began taking classes to work toward my GED. It was during these classes when I ran into a familiar face. It belonged to Freddy. My heart skipped a beat, and the biggest smile spread across my face. It had been so long since we had seen each other, but our conversation and that comfortable feeling did not miss a step. He told me he was still married but absolutely miserable. It seemed he felt the same way about his wife that I had felt about Andy for so long.

It did not take long for us to begin to spend time together and fall back in love with each other. I was willing to be with him, but I demanded that he get a divorce. If we were going to be together, I needed all of him. He complied quickly. His wife was bitter, but I think there was a mutual feeling of complacency in the relationship. We dated for a long time before I introduced him to my kids. He was a great father figure and incredibly romantic. The hugs, kisses, and touches were something I never had with Andy. The unexpected affection woke up my spirit. He moved in with me and helped support me and the kids. He kept a steady job but also sold cocaine. We would party together, snorting and drinking. However, his drinking was excessive. The new relationship and more frequent partying made my plans for school disappear. I felt like I did not need it now that Freddy came in and saved me.

All I ever wanted was to be chosen—chosen for good reasons, not reasons that I never agreed to. I did not want to be chosen to be picked on or chosen to fight others. I did not want to be chosen as prey to disgusting old men who chose me to use up and throw away.

I did not want to be chosen for a punching bag and be called names every waking moment. I wanted to be chosen for good. I knew there was good in me. Even when I tried to drown out the good with alcohol and numb it with coke, that good kept calling my name. I knew that good had to be God. I did not understand what God entirely meant. I assumed it had to be an all-or-nothing relationship with Him. How can God love someone who gets drunk, has sex, or does drugs? I had failed God. He could not possibly choose me for good. After the high was coming down and the people disappeared, I spent many nights crying to God and apologizing for how much I had failed Him. I was afraid of His punishment in my life, yet I continued to disobey.

I was stuck, caught in a net. I had no one to show me how to get on a right path. I had no idea of how to cope with being molested, raped, and beaten over and over again. That rage, that hate, and that sadness sat inside and rotted in me for so long. I was alone in this war. I was sure that other little girls were not passed around to men while their mother turned her head as if she did not notice. I was sure I was the only little girl who got pleasure from slicing her skin so that the sin-filled blood could find its only escape. I was sure that other little girls did not have beasts inside of them that tortured them so badly that drugs only slightly shut it up. The devil convinced me of these lies and kept me in loneliness. I knew that my problems did not matter and no one cared about my tears.

This loneliness is what kept me with Andy for so long, and it's also what kept me with Freddy. While Freddy treated me better than Andy, a switch would flip when he drank too much. The cocaine, we handled together, but when the alcohol flowed too much, his inner demon would come out and snap. I dealt with it. He was paradise compared to Andy, so when I woke up one morning with a diamond ring on my finger and him on his knee, I said yes. Our love was honest, flaws and all. We argued and fought and did drugs together. Doing drugs was a way of my romantic connection to him. But when that liquor got too deep into his system, his words became brutal to my heart. His words and actions hurt more than Andy's beatings because I was really in love with this man. So when he called me names, degraded me, and spit in my face, it tore my heart every single time.

Blacking out, trashing the house, throwing furniture, smashing glass, screaming names, and then binge-smoking crack—that was where Freddy took me. We were living in hell, a hell we created yet refused to change. I desperately wanted to change. I knew this was not me. Every time I got high, it only made me feel worse afterward. As desperately as I wanted to escape, I could not. I would get so high hoping to fade away and forget the horror, but it never did the task I intended it to, and a few times, I could not get high at all. It was like I was being warned, tested, but every time I would ignore that warning and fail that test, the disgrace I felt would flood me and make me feel like there was no coming back from it.

I escaped Andy to run into Freddy. I got away from one hell and entered another. Freddy was like Dr. Jekyll and Mr. Hyde. When sober, he was the most attentive and adoring man. He took me and my kids and treated them like they were their own. He was respectful, held down a decent job, and talked to me. When we were sober, we were best friends, best lovers and made pretty good parents. When Freddy would drink, it was like the darkness crawled out of his soul and filled his body. He became so disgusting in his mannerisms and hateful with his words. I have endured being disrespected and abused before, but his actions hurt so much more because I saw the potential of what could have been if the drugs and alcohol were not involved. I could not give up on him. I never felt such a connection with any man the way I have with him. I did not think I could change him, but I had hoped and prayed that I could inspire him to change himself. I was at a loss for what I should do. I despised not having a stable home or income to support me and my kids.

As much as Freddy hurt me, I did everything I could to stay with him. He was the lesser of the evils when compared to Andy. I had aspirations of becoming completely clean and getting some kind of an education, but those aspirations would never grow with Freddy. He was drowning, and by jumping in the water and trying to save him, he was drowning me.

The Case

My brother Redd lived with me most of his life once I moved out on my own. I continued to be his protector. He was gay but would not admit it to anyone but me for a long time. His lifestyle was hidden, and I think it created a bitterness within him. Hiding who you are all your life can be consuming. He always knew he could be himself around me. I was his safe place, his place of comfort. We were incredibly close through this bond. He knew my secrets, and I knew his. Redd got the nickname Redd early on as a kid because of his red hair. Redd was a bartender, and he would party as well. He, Freddy, and I would drink and snort coke and party at the bar then move the parties to the house afterward.

Redd witnessed a lot of the abuse I endured from Freddy. He did his best to keep me safe but was no match when it came to the violence that would occur. I would feel so incredibly guilty when he got involved. I was like Redd's mother, and I was supposed to protect him, not the other way around. One freezing Wisconsin Christmas eve, Redd and Freddy began drinking. I chose to not partake but watch TV with my youngest daughter instead. As the night got later and more liquor was consumed, I began to get nervous. I knew that Freddy was walking that fine line between a good time and all hell breaking loose.

That nervous feeling; that anticipation of darkness creeping up behind you; that feeling that life is fleeting and running and you are just trying to catch up to it; that feeling of fogginess, of forgetfulness, of amnesia because what you are about to see cannot be happening in reality; the feeling that you are in a movie, a play, a cartoon even because these things do not really happen—you know it is something huge, bigger than you can imagine, but it is not good. It is horrible. It is life changing.

That feeling was accurate. As the liquor increased, so did Freddy's temper. Before I knew it, he was enraged for some random, unimportant reason. He began picking up things around the house and smashing them. That was the usual routine for him: break and smash everything in the house before I became his victim. Vases, knickknacks, mirrors, pictures—everything would end up in pieces and litter the floor within a few minutes. One of the items flew across the room and shattered near my daughter's head. I jumped up and started screaming at him to calm down because he almost hit her. I demanded that my daughter go into her room. Just as she went in, Freddy picked up the heaviest vase we had and smashed me with it in the skull. The weight and strength knocked me out cold, and I slumped to the floor.

Redd could hear all the yelling, the breaking of glass, so he came to see what was going on. He saw me lying on the ground and was enraged at the thought of Freddy possibly killing me. He began to fight with Freddy. Redd was no match. Freddy picked up a chair and smashed it over Redd and bruised his face. With the thought of me being dead and him being next, Redd grabbed a butcher's knife from the kitchen, and when Freddy went to hit him, Redd stabbed him in the back. Redd ran out of the house to the payphone on the corner and dialed 911 for Freddy.

I woke up and saw that Freddy was stabbed, but I was furious about him beating me and my brother and the fact that my daughter was there. As I was yelling and screaming at him, he continued to bleed out. Freddy was coughing up blood and unable to move; I stared. At that moment, I did not care. I did not care that he needed help. I did not care that he was about to die. As horrible as it sounds, I was waiting for it. It was not until my small daughter came to me, begging "Mama, we need to help him! We need to go to the hospital!" with tears streaming down her face. I snapped out of my anger and loaded him and my daughter into the car and sped to the hospital.

As we flew down the street, I finally saw the police cars and ambulances heading in the direction of our house. We rushed into the emergency room parking lot and got out, but Freddy collapsed to the ground, and I couldn't carry him. I ran into the hospital with my daughter and screamed that he was outside on the ground bleeding and needed help. During our fight, Freddy doused me with liquor. So this was all you can smell on me even though I was not drinking. Immediately, the officers separated my daughter and me to begin their questioning. The police doubted my story because they assumed I was drunk. I told the truth, and yet I was treated like I did something wrong.

Soon after, I learned that while Redd stabbed Freddy in the back, he succeeded in puncturing a lung, and his lung collapsed. He was put on a ventilator, and the doctors did not think he would survive. This was the man that I loved despite his struggles and flaws. I truly felt that we were soul mates. The good times with him always outweighed the bad times, and now with a clear head, I did not want him to die. I sat in that waiting room, hysterically crying, thinking that I would never see Freddy alive again. I then began to think about Redd. The police arrested him. He was going to be charged with murder on my behalf. This whole horrific situation was my fault. My whole life, I felt I deserved every abuse, every rape, and every mistreatment at this point in my life. I have not been obeying God. I felt like absolute scum. I did not deserve for God to love me. How could He love me? I'm a whore, a drug addict, a horrible mother and person. I was responsible for Freddy possibly dying and my brother possibly going to prison. I was at a complete loss for the direction of my life. Do I even continue with this life? Freddy's family began their death threats to me and my family because of what happened to him. I was fearful that something might happen to Redd or my own kids in retaliation. I could not live with myself if something happened to them because Freddy's family was mad at me. I would rather they just hurt me instead.

After Redd was given stitches and medical care, he was taken downtown to the police station and charged with attempted murder. By the grace of God, Freddy survived and woke up. When he woke up, God must have spoken to his heart because he dropped the pending charges against Redd. I believe he knew he was in the wrong for what happened. After this unbelievable mess and addiction, Redd and I decided we needed a fresh start, a new lease on life. We wanted to get sober. I wanted to have my family back together. We decided to go to Missouri where my brother and my son were living. We needed to detox, to leave the environment we were in because it was filled with drugs and alcohol, and I knew deep down that I did not want this life anymore.

Redd and I got to Missouri while my two girls stayed back in Milwaukee with my mom until I could get a place for all of us. We lived with my brother Sam and his family and found a decent job. It only took three months before I got into a nice home in a good neighborhood for me and my kids. I filled it with furniture and all the household goods needed for my family. I was excited. I felt accomplished. I was off drugs and finally feeling free of addiction. As soon as my home was furnished, I sent for my girls to join me. My son was living back with me, and my daughters seemed to be adjusting well to the new surroundings.

While in Missouri, Freddy was constantly contacting me. He recovered from the injury fine. But his conversations consisted of apologies and begging for me to come back. He promised he would stop drinking. He reminded me over and over again of how long we had known each other and that I know he has a good heart when he is not on alcohol or drugs. He promised to do everything he could do to change and have all of us to be a family again. If it were true that a heart had strings, he pulled every single one of them. I loved this man deeply, but I was also so hurt by what had happened. I was at a crossroads. I have been the underdog all my life, so I cannot help but root for another when I see them. I was still so in love with him and missed him painfully, but I knew that as long as he was getting high and drunk, we would never be successful together. I gave him a proposition. I told him that I was not coming to him, but if he came to Missouri to be with me and remained sober, we could work it out.

In my mind, he was not coming. He said he was, but I thought that he would just continue to do what he's been doing in Milwaukee and I would soon be an afterthought. Surprisingly, he came to me. A new home, a new state, and a new, sober environment were what we needed. It did not take long for Freddy to find a good job, and the love I knew was deep under all the drugs and alcohol came to the surface. We were in love again, and our love was stronger than ever, so we finally decided to get married. I was twenty-nine years old and was married to the man I had been in love with since I was a teenager. We had been through hell together, and now I was ready to be happy with my husband.

We lived happily in Missouri and were married for two years before I suspected something strange. He would say he was working late or picking up shifts when really he was not there. I found out he was having an affair with a coworker, and he even started hiding the fact that he was drinking again. As if my heart could not break anymore, the pieces that were healed ripped open again. As much as everything was being stacked against me, I somehow found the strength to pursue. I have to believe that people can change because I so desperately want to change.

We decided to move back to Milwaukee to, hopefully, work on our marriage. As much as he had done to me, I could not give up on our love, on our family, or on our marriage.

We returned to Milwaukee and got established in a house down the street from Freddy's parents. We were healthy for a while. We went to church as a family, and we stayed clean, but after only seven months there, the temptations got the best of us, and we were right back where we started. That house was a beautiful house, and I loved it, but we turned it into a party house. We constantly had traffic in and out of other addicts whom we sold dope to and did dope with. I did not want my youngest daughter around the environment. My son went to live in Missouri with my brother Sam since he was twelve. He was growing into a young man, and I knew that Freddy or Andy could show him how to be a man. My oldest daughter having her own place, I signed over temporary custody to my oldest daughter. I had failed them as a mother, but I did not want them around for what else could possibly happen with all the drug addicts and dealers coming in and out of our home. I knew that I had a hell of a fight coming my way if I ever wanted to survive this environment.

I knew deep down, something was terribly wrong. Physically, I was tired all the time. I was a young woman but felt like I was trapped in an elderly body. I needed naps every day. Every outing, just sucked the energy out of me. I was sick all the time. I thought it was due to the constant drugs, but something inside of me kept growing and consuming me more than the need for drugs. Freddy was only attentive when he was sober, which became a rare occurrence. I could feel my life slipping away and the resentment from my kids growing. As they got older, they got wise to the fact that their mother was a drug addict. I knew they hated me. I had failed them just as my mother had failed me, only in a different way.

I did not want to give up on my marriage. As much as Freddy purposely used and hurt me, I knew that deep under the layers of ugliness, he was a good man. I had seen who he could be with God inside of him, and that was the man I longed for. Every time he hit me or called me names, I made excuses. I honestly felt that it was just the alcohol and drugs seeping into his soul and controlling his personality.

He was slowly changing from the man I fell in love with into a monster whom I despised. Still, I could not give up on him, and all I ever asked in return was to not be given up on, even when I felt I had given up on myself, even when I had thought God had given up on me. Somehow and someway, there had always been a way out. I had been, and am still to this day, a stubborn person. I have lived so long being independent and convinced that no one loved or even cared about me or my situation that when it was shown by people or from God, it has always been difficult for me to receive it. It was hard to find hope when all your life, you had been convinced that you are hopeless.

Vows

I never really had a good example of what a marriage was supposed to look like. I used men for what I needed, mostly finances, because those thoughts of real love and affection seem to die when grown men take advantage of little girls. I learned early on that sex can manipulate a man to do almost anything you needed him to do in that moment. When Jim and my mommy were married, he totally controlled her. She became this fake, robotic, creepier version of herself. He dominated her, and I hated her for letting him.

The irony was that I let Andy dominate me. I often wondered if Mommy was afraid of Jim the same way I was afraid of Andy and if that was why she became who he wanted as a wife. I wanted to marry Andy, but only because I wanted to have some kind of example of a real family for my kids. I now realize that by putting up with him so long, it only damaged and hurt my kids more. I was not sure of how a marriage worked, but I knew that when Freddy and I took those vows before God to be husband and wife, we both meant it.

In that moment, at that time, there was no doubt in my mind about this man's love for me. He proved it over and over again that I was worthy of love. He convinced me that we were soul mates, that we were best friends. In that moment, no one in the world could convince me that this man was not meant for me. This man had my best interest and happiness in mind at all times. This man would go to the ends of the earth just to be with me.

We got drunk together, got high together, and cleaned up and got sober together. We cried together, laughed out hardest together, and went to church. We prayed together and fought together. The end-all is that we were always together, and I just knew that not hell or high water could ever separate us.

Things have changed since then. That man I knew—that strong, brave, affectionate, romantic man—was gone. He had disintegrated. He let the sickness, the infection of addiction take over his mind, heart, soul, and body. I was no longer priority. His priority was scheming, plotting, cheating, and lying just to get to his next high. I was along for the ride, mostly because I did not want to be alone and I did not want to give up on my marriage. All I ever wanted was to do right, and that meant being and staying married. He was not perfect, but neither was I. Who could love these imperfections?

With my daughters and son out of our house, there was nothing left holding Freddy's anger back. The beatings got worse. Most of the fights were about drugs and money. If he could not get high or drunk, I became his punching bag. We were not only addicts; we were drug dealers, which was a contradicting combination. He hurt me relentlessly, both physically and emotionally. My self-esteem was nonexistent. He had thrown me to the ground and stomped me in my face. There was so much rage and hatred inside him that it grew, overflowed, and emptied onto me. On one of those many occasions, he called me names and hit me full force with a bat. He spit in my face, punched me in the stomach, and dragged me down the dark alley by my hair to what I was sure would be my death. He hit and choked me until all I saw was black. When I came to, I was actually disappointed. I just wanted it all to end. Why was I even here? To be tortured more? Hurt more? How much more would God allow to happen to me? I did not understand why I deserved all this. I did not understand how the man of my dreams turned into my nightmare.

Change

Change is hard. I have felt that my entire life has been just one change to another. Every time I anticipate a change for the better, I get hit with worse. I know now that change is growth; even when it is bad, it causes you to grow. During those changes, I did not see it as growth; I saw it as punishment. But then God gave me a good change, a blessing: my oldest daughter was pregnant. I was going to be a grandma.

My heart leaped. I never had a grandma, so I was so eager to be the best possible grandma I could be. But I could not be that person while on drugs. I could not give my grandbaby an addict as a grandmother. Things had to change. I knew it was going to be hard, and I was not sure that I would be successful, but I had to try my best to change. My grandbaby deserved better—better than what I received and even better than what my own children received. This was a new generation, a new chance, a new change.

Change usually doesn't happen without something strong behind it. The love for my grandbaby was strong, but Freddy's love for drugs was strong as well. During one of his enraged beatings, he threw me out of the house and locked the door and would not allow me in. It was a night of a horrible storm, and I stood there for a while, letting the rain wash over me. I was down so low I felt that God Himself could not see me. I was a complete failure—a failure to God, a failure as a mother, a failure as a wife, and I knew that my future grandbaby did not deserve someone like me. I was done. It was over. I had no control of men raping, molesting, and beating me, but I had control over this. I no longer wanted to live. The world, my kids, my grandbaby would be better off without me damaging them and inconveniencing them anymore.

I walked. I walked in the storm. The storm erupting above matched how it was erupting inside of me. As the clouds released its rain, my eyes released their tears. As the thunder boomed and cracked the sky, the thunder boomed my mind and cracked my heart. There was no point. Whatever happens, when I die, it had to be better than this life I was in. I walked to my mommy's house. By now she had been married to Myron for years. I walked into her house, past her questions and his annoying yelling, straight into her bathroom. I opened the medicine cabinet and swallowed every pill I could find. I did not know what I was taking, nor did I care.

I just hoped that it did the job. Handfuls of multicolored pills went down my throat. I ignored the pounding at the bathroom door and sank to the floor; smothered in my tears, I prayed. I prayed that through my mistakes and addictions, God let me into heaven. I prayed that this all be like a bad dream and I wake up in a better, more fair place, a place unlike this world. As my eyes closed and the calm sedation washed over me, I thought I was on my way to that place.

That place never came. Instead, I awoke in the hospital. The medical staff was able to get the pills out of my system and stabilize me. They also notified me that I would have to stay in the mental institution for a number of days to sort out my behaviors and feelings and possibly find the appropriate medication for me. This was a nightmare. I did not want to be interrogated about my childhood and all the horrendous things that happened to me. I tried my best to bury them, so to confess them to a stranger was not an option for me. All the doctors did was sedate me so that I could not cause problems or hurt myself further during my stay. They were all fake, with plastic smiles, and their concerns for my well-being were only part of the facade. I told the therapists whatever I think they want me to say in order to escape the asylum as soon as I can. Just as seductive I could be with my body, I could do the same with my words. They believed me; I was released.

I was released but not free. I had nowhere to go, so I ended up living back in hell with Freddy. I began to feel that sickness inside of me get stronger over time. I was weaker and losing weight. People began to notice my weight loss and just spread rumors about how strung out I was when I was the opposite at that time. I was too sick to even try to get high. Freddy had no concerns about my illness. He kept doing what he wanted. He wanted his drugs, he wanted his alcohol, and he wanted women other than his wife.

I noticed a mass on the side of my neck, and I felt God warn me that something was wrong. I had been fatigued and sick for years, but doing cocaine and pills and drinking, I thought, were to blame. They masked it, but they were not to blame. I knew something was wrong with my health. I went to the doctor, who recommended a surgical biopsy to remove it and test it. I know that with my past suicide attempts, it makes no sense that I was scared, but I was. After a few days, I went back for the results, and the physician said he had both good and bad news. Thankfully, the good news was that it was not cancer. The bad news was that I have a rare blood disorder called Castleman disease. The doctor explained that this disorder weakens the immune system, making me more susceptible to illness. At the same time, it can cause cancer cells in my blood, which can build up in my lymphatic system and cause lymphoma. I had to have surgery to have the lump in my neck removed. I'd needed scans and blood work often to keep track of my cell counts.

I was confused, baffled, and mortified. I knew something was wrong all this time, but I just blamed it on the drugs. I dropped out of school so young that the big words the doctor was using totally bypassed my brain and all I heard was a death sentence. I had no clue as to what to do next. That moment passed so slowly, but my life was going so fast. How was I going to tell my kids? What would become of my life?

During the doctor's visit, Freddy was listening and heard the conversation. He heard that the outcome could likely lead to cancer. His face dropped, and tears streamed down his face. He immediately stood up and left me in the exam room by myself to digest the news. He had no support for me. My mind was in a tailspin. I did not understand what the doctor was trying to explain to me. My anxiety was sky-high, and all I wanted to do was run out of that office, out of that building as fast as I could. My world crumbled in that moment, and my husband had left my side.

It was an endless cycle. I would be sick, vomiting, and exhausted, and I knew it was because of this disease, but I tried to cover it up with drugs. I would break it off with Freddy, but as soon as I came back to him, I came back to the drugs. I knew that while I was with him, there was no way I was going to be sober, there was no way I was going to gain control over this illness, there was no way I was going to live.

I had to finally make up my mind to leave. He did not care about me. His love for drugs overtook his love for me. I now had a beautiful grandbaby on the way to live for. I needed to be there for her birth, and the possibility of a part of me being reborn was all the motivation I needed to finally face my demon of addiction and make up my mind and heart.

Jesus, Help Me

When my daughter went into labor, I was there to see my gorgeous, perfect granddaughter be born. It was an almost out-of-body experience. I hated the pain my daughter was in. If I could trade places with her and take on that pain for her, I would have. I was helpless at that moment. As every mother, it is just their time to find that inner strength that they probably never knew they were capable of, but they have it all along. I had it all along—not just the strength to give birth, but the strength to get over my addiction, the strength to be healthier and live. Staring at that beautiful, angelic face filled me with so much hope. I knew it was not going to be just as easy as childbirth. I was going to have to face my pains, my labor head-on, but I knew I would rejoice and thank God for the birth of my sobriety, the birth of my new life.

I had called my brother Sam, who was still living in Missouri, and begged for him to let me come to finally get away from Freddy and get clean. I had to escape my environment if this was going to be successful. I did not leave Freddy in the dark. He knew how sick I was. I came to him with tears streaming down my face and begged him to come with me so that we could get clean together and possibly save our marriage. He cried too. The dilemma was written on his face. He said he would, but when the time came to leave and he knew I was serious, he refused to come with me.

I was crushed, heartbroken. He kept a piece of me with him as I packed a couple of bags, leaving all my other possessions behind, and got on that train to Missouri. Sitting in that seat, looking out the window, I watched the world pass by. I could not believe that as much as Freddy claimed to have loved me, he was not willing to give

73

up drugs and alcohol to be with me. I did not even want him to do it for me; I wanted him to do it for himself. He was not happy, and he sure was not healthy. Whether we were together or not, I still had so much love for him, and I prayed that he would find a happier, more fulfilling life than looking for his next high or his next drink every day. I felt unchosen by him but definitely chosen by God. Under all the ugliness I was feeling and the horrible guilt, I knew that God had to be on my side; otherwise, I would have been dead a long time ago.

I arrived to Missouri and moved in with my brother. I wanted to go back home so bad. I missed my husband, I missed my kids, and I missed my granddaughter so much. I felt like I had failed them so many times. The devil has a way of making you beat yourself down into a hole that you can barely see the light out. But that light was there, and it was Jesus. I got on my knees and, with tear-filled eyes, prayed that He keep me strong; I prayed that He would help me get over Freddy. I prayed and apologized for being an addict and asked to be broken free. I missed them so much, but I knew I was not strong enough emotionally or spiritually to go back.

After eight months of taking care of my mind and soul, I felt I could go back and face what I left. I came back to Milwaukee and moved in with my mother until I could get on my feet, but I immediately filed for divorce from Freddy. My divorce attorney told me that legally, I deserved many things from our ten years together. I could have gotten the car, house, furniture, and money, but I settled with nothing. I wanted nothing from him but him out of my life. I learned through God to forgive him, and I prayed that he would wake up, but soon after I left him, he moved in with another woman and kept doing the same activities. He was not going to change.

Loner but Not a Loser

Soon after my divorce was final, I won some money at the local casino, enough to finally get on my feet. I was able to get my own place to live and buy a car. I got my youngest daughter, Alexis, back living with me, and my granddaughter was over a lot. I was content, but realizing that I had no friends made for lonely times. All my friends were still addicts, and I could not risk being around them, thinking I could resist the temptation of relapsing. My brother Redd was partying and getting high all the time, and out of everyone, I wanted him to stop the most. He got even more strung out while I was in Missouri getting cleaned up, and he was clearly thinner and sicker. I offered to go with him to Missouri for a while so that he can get clean, but every time the topic came up, he had an excuse. It killed me to watch my best friend slowly disintegrate before my eyes.

As soon as I got back to Milwaukee, the streets were talking. All my so-called friends and a lot of family began to gossip about me. They doubted my sobriety and made up stories about seeing me getting drugs from dealers or seeing me high. At first, it bothered me; it boiled me. How was anything I did their business? It seemed that they wanted me to look horrible in order to make their situation, their addiction not as bad. I got used to it after a while; after a while, I did not even care. Those closest to me knew me. And most importantly, God knew me. God was whom I was accountable to and had to answer to. I had many lonely moments or that feeling like I was missing the fun, missing the party. But then I had to sit back and ask myself if it was worth it. Going backward was not worth it. Losing the relationship I was finally trying to build with my kids was not worth it. My health was not worth it.

Nothing to Numb
Me Now

All the traumatic events were blurred by the smoke of crack, of weed, by swallowing pills and alcohol. Now that those things had been purged from my life, the blurry events had gotten clearer. My nights were filled not with restful, peaceful sleep but with a battle. It was a battle of demons coming for me, dreams of me getting high again. I woke up screaming, crying and in tears often. There were constant flashbacks of Butch, Harry, and others touching me, breathing on top of me, raping me. The feelings of being spit on, slapped, punched, and thrown against walls by men I thought loved me were becoming clearer and clearer the more sober I got.

I could not escape it. I spent so many years in a fog trying to numb it, trying to forget it; now that there was nothing to numb it, I had to face it. The only way I knew how to face anything that scared me even as a little girl was to pray. My relationship with God had always been rocky. I never felt I deserved His love or forgiveness, but I knew that He had strength, and I knew that I had to lean on Him when I had none. I could not face my past without Him.

From the outside, no one believed I was serious about being off drugs. Everyone assumed I was lying. When I ran into past dealers, they would always offer a discount, and as tempting as it was at times, I kept the thought of my kids and grandbaby in mind, and I refused to go back.

Everyday Battle

As I was growing up, the concept of God, of Jesus had always been hard for me to understand. I was surrounded by so many people who claimed to be Christians and faithful, yet they did awful, horrible things. As I grew up, I knew that the only one I had to lean on in this lifetime would be Jesus. Even though my mother scared us as children by talking about the wrath of God, I learned that Je is all-loving and forgiving as well. He has to be forgiving of me. That thought was all I had to hold on to during my sobriety.

I am far from perfect, but I admit my mistakes. In the beginning of my sobriety, I did fail a few times, but each time, my entire heart and soul filled with guilt. It came to a point that I could not even feel the high because God was in my heart and it did not feel like my purpose any longer. Jesus is my crutch, and whenever I doubted Him, He showed me in ways I could not even describe that He is real and He is listening to my cries.

As I grew as a child of God, I also grew as a mother and grandmother. I regretted the decisions I made, and I hated that I put my family through so many horrible experiences, but I was determined to be better. I was determined to help my brother Redd. He was in horrible shape, still using drugs and out all night partying. I begged him to get clean, and I told him that if Jesus can help me, there was hope for him. He was my best friend, and I was his protector, but I could not save him myself. I tried to keep him with me to avoid all the old people I knew who used. It was my job to make sure he was okay, and he was not.

As my sobriety got stronger, my health problems became more prevalent. I had to keep up with seeing my oncologists, getting CT scans and routine blood work. Having multiple appointments and meeting person after person made my anxiety fly sky-high. I had walked right out of waiting rooms in full panic attacks because of the fear of being judged. I did not know how to exchange properly in conversations. My vocabulary was limited, and explaining my emotions was a skill I lacked. My health was important to me, but it was a whole overwhelming mountain to climb in order to be mentally and emotionally ready for the never-ending battle.

Multiple times I felt belittled, made fun of, and so incredibly stupid. My mouth dried up, my legs and hands shook, and all I could think about was running away from all these people instead of asking the important questions that I would have later. It was not a treatment; it felt like an interview every time, and I never felt good enough.

It was a twisted cycle that left me confused, scared, and feeling alone. I never knew where to start and when it would ever end. I tried to keep up with the testing and appointments, but mentally and physically, I just could not keep up. I did know that overall, it was important, and no matter how much I had wanted to die in my past, I knew that it was not for me to determine, and I knew that I wanted to live.

Heartbroken

Inside of me, there was a pit of doubt, confusion, and fear. It was an intuition, an inclination of what was to come. I felt that God was preparing me for something bad, and I knew it. Redd was just getting worse, losing weight, and not taking care of himself like he would normally. I knew that he had let his addiction take over the things that previously made him smile.

God has shown me many things over the years through visions and dreams. He warned me of my own death, but then He also warned me of Redd's. He vividly showed me signs of what was to come, and it was so clear that I woke with sweat down my face and tears down my cheeks. I wanted to deny it, but it was not just a dream; it was premonition.

He slowly lost that fire in his eyes. That loud laugh began to quiet. His personality changed. Despite everything we went through together as kids, he had always had an uplifting view on life. He got me through many extremely hard times and refused to let me doubt myself. I just wanted to do the same in return. He was my brother, and I still felt like I needed to protect him. So when he was diagnosed with kidney failure and told that he would need dialysis a few times a week, he moved in with me. His cycle of drug use and being properly medically treated was a never-ending, winding path. He would do great for a couple of weeks, stay clean, go to dialysis, and even look healthy. But there were too many times that he would skip treatments and be missing because he was most likely at the local dealer's house on a binge. By the time he came to me, he would be swollen, sick, and on the verge of death. I would help get him to dialysis in time to get the excess fluid and poison out of him.

It was extremely difficult to watch my brother, whom I love so much, slowly decay. I had to put my own health care on the back burner because my brother needed me. He needed my help. As he was living as a gay man with no longtime partner, wife, or kids, all he had was me. It was my duty. Every day watching him so weak from dialysis lying on my couch slowly disintegrated my heart. I desperately clung to him and who he used to be.

He suffered a severe stroke after one of his drug binges. He was in a coma for a short while, and when he awoke, as much as the drugs stole his personality, the stroke completely rid him of it. He was not himself at all. He was skin and bones, hooked up to hoses and machines. He contracted MRSA by being in the hospital for so long, so he was in an isolation room. Every time I would visit him and gown up, I hated the bander between my hand and his hair as I stroked it. I would hold his hand and talk to him, try to uplift him the way that he would do me.

Once the hospital deemed him stable, they wanted to move him to a nursing home. Redd was not rich; he depended on state assistance, and when you depend on the state, you have to do what the state tells you to do. They moved him hours away in Waukegan where it would be a long trip or so to get to him. I visited, and my heart was destroyed. He was not being taken cared of the way he would have been had he been at home. His hair was uncombed; his teeth were unbrushed. He was completely mentally incapacitated. He would recognize me one second and forget who I was the next. He was bone thin and had to be transported by wheelchair. He was wasting away before my eyes, and I prayed I would wake up from the nightmare.

This was not a nightmare; it was reality, and I could not escape from it by waking up. Redd was always so well put together. He stayed clean, smelling good, and he took pride in his hygiene. If he saw himself the way I saw him in that nursing home, he would be ashamed and angry. I felt ashamed and angry for allowing my brother to be treated this way. As a family, as his sister, I felt stuck. No one had money to afford better care for him, and it broke my heart.

It was not long before Redd suffered an additional stroke and I became his power of attorney for health care. The physicians tending to his health sat me down in a cold big conference room and told me that my sweet, smart, funny brother had suffered irreversible brain damage and that hospice care was recommended; because of the damage, he did not have long. I can only describe it as an out-of-body experience. I was hearing the words that they were saying, but I do not think I comprehended them. It was not until I saw his frail body in the hospice bed clinging to life that it all was reality. If there was ever a moment when I felt like putting a pipe in my mouth and getting high, it was now. Day after day, I came to see him; I rubbed his scalp and held his hand. I prayed, asking God if I was making the right decision by him. I knew God performed miracles, and doctors never had the final say, but I also knew that despite my efforts and the efforts of many physicians, if God was calling my brother home, then I could not fight that will.

Our mother was there with him and prayed over him while he took his last breath. In that moment, I did not understand. I did not understand why he suffered so much before finally passing away. All the procedures, all the medications, all the treatments seemed to do no good and only cause more pain and problems for him.

I did not understand why God did not just take him right away. Why so much time? I now have to believe that God granted him that time for a reason. I have to believe that during that time, Redd was forgiven of his sins and prepared to be welcomed into heaven. I have to believe that God was preparing Redd's place there with Him and that suffering and time were well worth the reward.

Dealing with his funeral was a whole other fight and battle. I came to peace that he was no longer suffering, but I missed him so much. He was my best friend. When anything good or bad happened in our lives, we always had each other to run to. My comfort was gone. I missed his loud laughing and his great sense of humor and outlook on life. He was a huge light in my life that had slowly dimmed out and now left me in the dark. I was left putting together the pieces of his funeral arrangements. Meeting with the funeral home representative and picking out a coffin were like shopping in a death store. The overly pleasant and friendly mood of the representative unmatched the feelings of depression and anxiety I had inside and made me even more uncomfortable.

I pushed through and stayed strong for him. We decided on a closed coffin; we all knew Redd no longer looked like himself upon his death, and we did not want anyone remembering him in that condition. That disease, that state of mind was not him in any shape or form. I had to be medicated with antianxiety medication during his funeral in order to keep from walking out and having a total breakdown. Seeing everyone we knew from the time we were kids show up and pay their respects was something out of a dream or, rather, a nightmare.

You never truly get over a death of someone you loved so much. I thought dealing with Laura's death would be the worst of it, but Redd dying took a huge part of me that can never be replaced. I just learned to deal every day with the hurt and pain of missing him so deeply. Nothing could ever fill the void that he left behind. As much as our mother acted as if she hated Redd at times, I know that his death traumatized her as well. It can never be easy being at the side of your son as he takes his last breath.

The only thing holding me together is God. He's always been the one holding me together. I always wondered why He saved me so many times, but now I know that I have a purpose. I'm not always sure of what it is or how it is going to work out, but I do know that there is no way I am supposed to be alive today.

Purpose?

For as young as I can remember, I have always felt unloved, abandoned like a piece of trash thrown out a car window and left on the side of the road. I felt unworthy of anything good or loving. I felt misunderstood, alone, and deeply sad. Even when family would try their best to convince me that they loved me, I had the devil in my head telling me that they were lying. I felt like everyone was fake, they masked who they really were. They claimed love, but evil lurked below the surface.

These feelings would periodically spin me into a deep, demonic depression. Those thoughts, those doubts and fears would play on repeat in my mind. No one really cared whether I lived or not; I would not be missed. It consumed me to the point that I would think of different ways to end my life. I would obsess about it. Someone could say something negative to me that, in their mind, was not a big deal, but in my possessed mind, it was a trigger; it was a sign confirming that I did not deserve to live.

The first time I tried to end my life, I was around eleven years old, around the time Mommy married Jim. I found some unknown pills and swallowed a handful of them. I passed out and woke up in the hospital. I don't think I actually wanted to die. Sadly, I wanted attention. Attention from my mommy would have meant the world to me, but that never came. As I'm looking back at it now, it was definitely a cry for help because the incidents after became more aggressive. I wanted to do it the "right way."

I'd tried to take my life a few times and, sadly, was disappointed to wake up. I did not want this life. Nothing could be worse than this feeling. Nothing could be worse than the voices in my head torturing me. Nothing could be worse than being a disappointment to my children. Nothing could be worse than every man I have been with hurting me, beating me, and disrespecting me without thought.

Something had to be better about death. I craved that peace. It was harder and harder to find the strength.

I have peace now. God has helped me realize that He is present in my life and has never left me even when everyone else has. My life is in His hands, not mine. Every day is a struggle. It was a struggle to forgive all those in my life who had hurt me or had done me harm. It was a struggle to be alone with my thoughts. It was a struggle to recognize which thoughts were the demons and rebuking them. It was also a struggle to allow Raulph back in my life when he got out of prison.